Journey to Makkah

Journey to Makkah

Murad Hofmann

Translated from German by
Andreas Ryschka

amana publications
Beltsville, Maryland

First Edition
(1419AH / 1998AC)

10 09 08 07 06 05 04 03 02   9 8 7 6 5 4 3 2 1

© Copyright 1419AH / 1998AC
amana publications
10710 Tucker Street
Beltsville, Maryland 20705-2223 USA
Tel: (301) 595-5777 / Fax: (301) 595-5888
E-mail:amana@igprinting.com
Website: www.amana-publications.com

Library of Congress Cataloging-in-Publication Data

Hofmann, Murad Wilfried 1931 (1350) —
    [Reise nach Makka. English]
    Journey to Makkah / by Murad Wilfried Hofmann.
        p.   cm. 23
    Includes bibliographical references and index.
    ISBN 0–915957–85–X
    1. Hofmann, Murad Wilfried--Journeys--Saudi Arabia-Mecca.
2. Muslim pilgrims and pilgrimages--Saudi Arabia--Mecca. 3.Mecca
(Saudi Arabia)--Description and travel. I. Title.
DS248.M4H6413   1998
297.3'52'092--dc21
[B]   98-31079
                                                                  CIP

Printed in the United States of America by
International Graphics
10710 Tucker Street
Beltsville, Maryland 20705-2223 USA
Tel: (301) 595-5999 Fax: (301) 595-5888
E-mail: ig@igprinting.com
Website: igprinting.com

Contents

PREFACE

With my previous book *Islam: the Alternative,* I attempted to refute a large number of unfounded prejudices against individual aspects of Islam. No wonder this publication virtually turned into a textbook on the theory, doctrine, and norms—legal and moral—of that religion.

Journey to Makkah is different. It was written when my German publisher sent me a contract for a (yet unnamed) book which would not, like the first one, deal with the great spiritual idea, theory, and edifice of Islam but with Islam in practice: What happens when one tries to live that religion, and how others react to it.

In line with that, this book does not celebrate the self-perception of Islam as a grand, universally valid project for all human society and all of its members. Rather, it copes with some down-to-earth aspects, the not so elating realities which one may encounter as a "practicing Muslim" (even with oneself), given that people, are people, are people.

Since all religions demand a great deal of their followers, in terms of self-sacrifice, discipline, compassion, altruism, fraternity, justice, honesty, and other ethical and moral virtues, it does not come as a surprise that many followers, in all religions, do not live up fully to their ideals. In this respect, no religion (or ideology at that) is entitled to throw the first stone.

But when Muslims find themselves entangled in un-Islamic traditions or when they are too weak to live up to the ideals of their faith, they still know that they are doing wrong, and usually do not look for a disclaimer. Islam remains the mirror on their wall.

It is my hope that this book will help to demonstrate that Islam continues to be a force capable of reforming people to an astonishing degree, actually causing individual moral revolutions: how much strength Muslims can derive from their faith and to which enormous degree the Muslim world has absorbed Islam, once and, I hope, for all.

Murad Wilfried Hofmann
Istanbul, August 1998

JOURNEY TO MAKKAH

After patiently waiting in line at Casablanca Airport, it was finally our turn at the counter. After checking in our scant luggage, the clerk casually suggested that we either return the 80 miles to Rabat, or while away the hours in Casablanca. This was his way of letting us know that the SAUDIA jumbo jet from Dakar, which had been expected to arrive here about an hour ago, had not even made it to Dakar yet. Under normal circumstances, such a situation would have likely sparked resentment, even protest. However, all of the passengers—the majority of them women—were pilgrims bound for Makkah, ever mindful of the Qur'an's admonition:

> Let there be no sexual relations, nor sin, nor dispute during the Hajj. (2:197)

It is a pilgrim's highest duty to exercise patience, and to nip any impending quarrel in the bud. He must not injure anybody or anything, not even pluck a leaf of grass, or kill a mosquito. Therefore, the mood at the counter remained quite civilized and quiet.

Eventually, the departure was postponed from the evening of May 28, to early the following morning. But among the pilgrims no one was about to leave the Mohammed V terminal. Who was going to risk missing the most important flight of his life? Everyone of us had already received the traditional farewell visits from our friends and neighbors, which served to remind everybody that in the old days a Moroccan's 8,000 miles long round-trip to the holy sites in the Hijaz would last as long as a year, and that for many a pilgrim this would be a journey without return. Indeed, we were not going to return to Rabat except as *hujjaj*—as Muslims who had fulfilled their duty to pay a visit to the "House of God" (*Bayt Allah*) in Makkah.

During prayers in the evening and on the following morning, Casablanca airport turned into a vast, sprawling mosque encompassing the departure

1

terminal, the salon d'honneur, even extending to the first class lobby. It was touching to see how a farmer's wife from the Rif mountains was looking after her blind husband. His ardent prayers were exemplary. A blind seer indeed! In the meantime, we were wearily and silently scouring the terminal for food. A young Saudi sitting at my table exclaimed all of a sudden, "Whenever I travel there are times when I'm tempted to drink alcohol. Then I always remind myself: After all, you're from Makkah!" Remembering many an inebriated Saudi businessman or diplomat, I wish this nobility of spirit obliged everybody.

At long last, at 5:37 A.M., the Saudi Airlines Boeing 747 took off toward Jeddah, traversing the vast and empty deserts of Libya and Sudan. Instead of the sleep inducing whisper of the music, the speakers on board began with recitations from the Qur'an. In Dakar, a number of black pilgrims had boarded the plane. They were the most exemplary of exemplary pilgrims, with Mokhtar Diouri among them, a son of Senegalese President Diouf. Each and every one of them was radiating an aura of quiet bliss.

Half an hour before touchdown, the captain notified everybody that we were about to enter the air space around Makkah's Haram-district. Even way up in the skies, this area is restricted to pilgrims dressed in the appropriate attire. At this point, for those who expressed their intention (*niyyah*) to begin their actual pilgrimage, this was the signal to don the required garment (*ihram*). In no time at all, the entire plane seemed to have turned white. All the women were without veils and wearing long, white gowns covering their legs and arms, as well as white headscarves. The men were draped in whole pieces of 31/2 by 6 feet long white terrycloth slung around hips and shoulder.

I myself had not changed outfits yet, because Makkah was not going to be my first destination. I had planned first to make the "visit" (*ziyarah*), i.e., the visit to Muhammad's burial mosque in al Madinah ("the city," i.e., of the Prophet), before embarking on the ritual stage of my pilgrimage.

But my suitcase was already filled with all the things an aspiring *hājj* would need—everything had previously been obtained from the medieval suq in the ancient corsair city of Salé: the two large unsewn strips of terrycloth, the unsewn shoulder sack designed to carry a copy of the Qur'an along with an emergency ration of water, the white umbrella for sun protection, and the broad leather belt to secure the hip cloth, which is worn without anything underneath. The belt is stapled, not sewn together, and

2

offers the customary three inner pockets: one for passport and airline ticket, one for money, and one for medicine because we were only immunized against meningitis. Following the advice of my pilgrim-savvy family physician, I had packed an array of medical articles for the treatment of head and toothaches, stomach disorders, vomiting, diarrhea, fever, as well as band-aids for bruised and sore feet.

I also carried in my suitcase the traditional unsewn sandals. I had them cut, braided and glued by an old shoemaker in the bazaar of Salé. The venerable old man was half blind and looked like he might have well spent his entire life outfitting pilgrims. Alas, he was now, as I noticed much too late, not up to it anymore. As I was about to leave, his neighbor winked at me, took the botched-up sandals out of my hands, and without uttering a single word proceeded to fix them without the old man's knowledge, and without charging any money.

Among Jeddah's five airports, the pilot managed to get us into the right one. At least he was able to use the uniquely aesthetic, unforgettable silhouette of the pilgrims' terminal as a landmark for his approach. It is built from concrete, yet manages to evoke a tent city hovering above the desert sands.

After our arrival, my fellow 2.2 million pilgrims and I immediately found ourselves in the hands of a guide (*muṭawwif*), who is responsible for food, lodging, transportation, and in charge of strictly enforcing the rules of the hajj. This is certainly very reassuring, even after painstaking and almost talmudic study of Qur'an and Sunnah to memorize all the dos and don'ts, the when, where, how, and wherefores that a pilgrim has to master in order that his pilgrimage be acceptable to Allah. Allah willing.

In my hotel, which is run by Royal protocol, I met Muslims from all over the world—from the Comoro Islands to Washington, D.C. All our conversations centered in blissful variety around one single topic: Islam. Because of these intellectual exchanges, I soon began to experience my pilgrimage as a mobile university.

One of the people I had many discussions with was Shaykh Mahfoudh Naḥnaḥ from Algiers. In the course of my pilgrimage, he would be crossing my path time and again.

Journey to Makkah

*

On May 31, on its way to the military airport, our convoy was racing through Jeddah at such a maddening speed that one of our vehicles got completely left behind. We arrived early, only to spend the next 40 minutes in sweltering heat, waiting for the latecomers to catch up.

Didn't I point out that patience is the pilgrim's supreme virtue?

A short while later, a Saudi air force Hercules C130 took us on a 50-minute-flight into *al Madinah al Munawwarah* (the Illuminated City). It was here that Muhammad was granted asylum from his persecutors from Makkah. In Madinah, Islam became a State religion. Here, the Prophet dictated the first written constitution of a federal (Muslim-Jewish) State. And it was here that the Prophet of Islam taught the world and died.

Together with Shaykh Naḥnaḥ, I immediately left for the Prophet's Mosque. Originally, it had been constructed above Muhammad's compound, his living quarters and garden (*rawḍah*). Numerous times over the years the mosque has been enlarged in scale, based on original outlines, but the most recent expansion definitely eclipses all previous ones.

In 1982, on my last visit here, the mosque had six minarets; now there are 11, and three additional ones are in the planning. Back then, the mosque extended over one entire block, now it covers an entire section of the city—2.5 million square feet—and offers space to pray for 600,000 believers. Its great number of columns dwarfs the great Umayyad mosque in Cordoba.

The Madinah Mosque

4

An engineering firm run by German Muslims equipped the uncovered parts of the mosque with 50 ft wide giant parasols which automatically open and close according to sunlight and always direct themselves toward the course of the sun.

Under a simmering 108 °F, hundreds of thousands of people simultaneously converged on the mosque from all sides in order to perform the evening prayer at this blessed site. Even as those full-sized, air-conditioned American limousines carrying the more privileged pilgrims slowly make their way through the crowds, there are no curses, angry words, ugly gestures, or envious fists banging against the car. Even though the pilgrims are enjoined to peacefulness toward man, beast and plants, the general discipline among the crowds remains astonishing nonetheless. Before witnessing this, I would never have believed religious commandments to be capable of even so much as temporarily suspending the laws of sociology.

Praying by my side were a Pakistani banker from Bahrain, and a Turkish fellow who was working as a "guest worker" in Bochum, Germany. (Experiencing the universal presence of Islam first hand is also an integral part of the hajj.) Even considering the cooling effect of those giant parasols, we were amazed that the temperature inside was a mere 82 °F, although the mosque is open on all sides. Later, somebody explained to us that the Saudi government had lately begun to let ice-cold water circulate underneath the mosque. This water has to be routed here from miles away, otherwise, the energy released by the cooling process would bring this already over-heated city to the boiling point.

Around midnight we finally managed to visit the gravesites of the Prophet Muhammad and the first two caliphs, Abu Bakr and 'Umar, in the oldest part of the mosque. We lingered in the Prophet's former dwellings. On his burial site used to be the house of his very young, highly esteemed, and uncommonly intelligent wife 'A'ishah, to whom we owe many precise and down to earth reports about her husband.

To be standing at the very place where the highly revered, yet never deified Prophet lived, planned, preached, loved, and finally died is overwhelming to even the most cerebral among us. In the face of this intensely historical site, some of my fellow pilgrims broke out in tears, shaken as they were to the very core of their souls.

It was way past midnight when we left, and I saw that the Prophet's rather archaic, and supremely dignified prayer niche (mihrab) was still occupied

5

by a group of Malaysian women who seemed unable to bring their fervent prayers to an end. And yet nobody would even think about making them leave by so much as a glance at their watches, not even the impatiently waiting nightly cleaning crew.

Afterwards, we were having discussions with a group of Algerian students of Islamic sciences until it was time for morning prayers. We were at their place, a modest yet tidy "mattress-camp," which they called *"al nahḍah"* (the awakening)—pun (but also the political message) intended. The topic of our discussion is an easy guess. On my way there, I witnessed the enormous popularity enjoyed by my travel companion. Shaykh Naḥnaḥ could not walk 50 yards without Algerians coming up to embrace him, hail him, and ask him for advice.

The following day I visited the famous *Al Baqi'* burial grounds, where with the exception of Ḥamzah, the Lion of Islam, and the first two caliphs the Prophet's entire family is buried, together with those companions who died in Madinah. 'A'ishah, his wife, and his daughter Faṭimah—mother of the Prophet's grandsons Al Ḥasan and Al Ḥusayn—are among them. At the same time, there is no excessive cult over burial grounds or at shrines, quite in keeping with the principle against hero worshipping of original Islam which represents a stark contrast to Egypt and the Maghrib with their reverence for Muslim "saints." Quite the contrary, in 1982, the most important graves, such as Caliph 'Uthman's, were still recognizable. Now, however, the whole cemetery is leveled out in long waves, and no one can walk there anymore.

After each prayer, the bodies of the pilgrims who had passed away since the last prayer were carried into the mosque. We prayed for their souls, saddened only that they were unable to complete their hajj. Is there a more desirable end than dying in Makkah or Madinah? Did many a pilgrim not come here hoping to be allowed to end his days at this very place? I was fully aware that I could well be among those to be carried in next. The thought did not trouble me in the least.

Then we joined many other pilgrims on a trip to the two historical mosques, Quba' and Al Qiblatayn, and to Uhud battlefield, where Muhammad's uncle, Ḥamzah, is buried. Here the first Muslims learned an important lesson when, as a result of a lack in discipline, they suffered their only military setback and, in the course of which, Muhammad suffered

6

facial wounds. Today, Uhud is a drab, barren place, without any kind of helpful directions or explanations for interested visitors.

Unfortunately, the so-called historic mosques are anything but. The religious authorities in Saudi Arabia have a disdain for worldly things, as well as an abiding suspicion that reverence of things and people past might degenerate into idolatry (*shirk*). Therefore, both mosques have since been repeatedly and recklessly rebuilt and built over. In 1982, I was still able to see those niches in the "mosque with the two prayer niches" *(al qiblatayn)*: one was the original niche facing Jerusalem, and the other, equally pristine yet slightly younger, was facing Makkah. Standing here, it was easy to understand the impact on the Jewish-Muslim relationship after Muhammad, following a revelation he received during prayers, replaced Jerusalem with Makkah as the *qiblah*. It never bothered the Prophet that the old prayer niche was preserved. Only now, at the end of the 20th century, one begins to take exception. After the latest reconstruction efforts, neither of the two historical niches can be spotted anymore. With all that, it would have been easy to integrate the small and dignified Qiblatayn Mosque into the new and larger mosque, or simply to have built the new one over it.

On June 3, the Saudi Air Force took us back to Jeddah. Earlier, we had toured the world's most state-of-the-art book printing shop on the outskirts of Madinah. From here, 38 million copies of the Qur'an are annually distributed all over the world, among them millions in English, French, and even Korean translation. Every pilgrim receives his own personal copy.

This time, before boarding the plane, I took the formal resolution (*niyyah*) to carry out the pilgrimage in the two-part fashion recommended by the Prophet, the *hajj al tamattu'* (first *'umrah*, then, after interruption, hajj). I bathed, said the required prayers, donned belt, sandals and both strips of terrycloth. Thus attired, it was visible to everybody that shortly before driving to the airport I had formally entered the state of pilgrimage (*ihrām*).

Shortly before? Naturally we had been waiting for two hours for the limousine that would take us to the airport, and then another two hours for the departing flight. And yet nobody would even breathe a single word about it.

At that point, a number of Indians asked me to help them resolve a dilemma: As everybody knows, one leaves the state of pilgrimage by having at least a lock of hair cut off. However: since the prohibition of doing

7

harm to any living thing extends even to the cutting of one's own hair and fingernails, how could pilgrims release each other from their ritual state (*ihrām*)? My straight answer was: They can't. For that purpose, young boys with scissors at the ready are placed at strategic sites and are happy to swiftly oblige the pilgrim in return for a donation.

I had worn the pilgrim's attire before, for half a day, on my first *'umrah* (the brief pilgrimage), which I undertook in 1982, but I did not feel quite at ease yet in my terrycloth gown. The top strip kept slipping out of place but it protected me from sunburn, and the fabric absorbed the sweat, but in air conditioned rooms I easily began to shiver. The most important thing to remember is that all pilgrims, rich or poor, strong or weak, intelligent or ingenuous, young or old, are wearing the same attire. Since the strips of cloth must not have any kind of pattern and must not be sewn together, no individual can stand out by even so much as a neat seam. The pilgrim's gown not only symbolizes everybody's equality before God, it also evokes the Day of Judgment. As we were pacing back and forth in the airport lobby, we looked like resurrected souls still wrapped in their burial shrouds. As a matter of fact, many pilgrims do decide to keep their gowns for their own burial.

As the plane came rolling in toward the terminal, we could discern the figures of Madinah's protocol officers standing like imposing, aristocratic silhouettes on the edge of the tarmac. Every single gesture, their very steps were majestic, measured and controlled. They are all tall in stature, with aquiline noses and neat, closely cropped beards defining their noble features. Airy cloaks, black with golden borders, bestow a touch of royal elegance on these men. What a contrast to us people in shrouds!

My fellow pilgrims from Senegal, who were on the Hercules with me, felt particularly sensitive about Arabs who, following the Jewish example, seemed to consider themselves a chosen people. This is particularly true for the rare Quraysh from Makkah, and the tribes around Madinah, but they are by no means the only ones. I will concede that hitting it big twice in the course of history can easily go to one's head. First of all, the last of the prophets, the "seal" of all revelation, appeared in Arabia with a message in Arabic; and secondly, there are the blessings of oil and natural gas reserves. (Blessings?) In spite of that, nobody on the airplane was ready to accept the conclusion that Arabs alone were capable of comprehending the divine message in every respect. On that score, we all considered a two-class society incompatible with Islam.

The noise in the machine made such discussions far too difficult, but could not keep us from joining into the call of the pilgrim *(talbiyah)*, as so many of our predecessors had done for the last 1400 years before us: *Labbayka, Allahuma labbayk; labbayka lā sharika laka, labbayk; inna al hamda wa an-niᶜmata laka wa l-mulk; lā sharika lak!* (Here I stand before You, O Allah, here I stand, here I stand before You, there is no other god but You, here I stand before You; Thine is all the praise, the grace and the power; there is no other god but You.)

Until the upcoming Festival of Sacrifice *('Id al Aḍhā)* I would constantly hear someone around me recite this prayer—if only myself.

That day we also learnt the precise date of the Festival because the new moon of the month of pilgrimage (Dhu al Ḥijjah) was visible in the night. This meant that the day of 'Arafat would fall on June 10, with the Festival of Sacrifice following on June 11. We were entering home stretch.

*

On June 4, I performed the first part of the *hajj al tammatu'*, the rites of the *'umrah*. I was accompanied on this occasion by Sri Lanka's Minister of Islamic Affairs, A.H.M. Azwer, and his family. The fact that we spent the entire afternoon and parts of the evening waiting for transportation from Jeddah to Makkah was quite propitious, because when we finally did arrive there, the local temperature had already fallen to 100 °F. We were passing through one of the tunnels that had been driven through the bedrock of *Makkah al Mukarramah* (the Honorable Makkah) and were completely taken by surprise when upon emerging from the ground we suddenly found ourselves right in front of the magnificent *Masjid al Haram*. I was overwhelmed!

Here we stood, in the tradition of Abraham, in front of the world's oldest monotheistic temple, the Ka'bah. It is a cube with walls that are crudely constructed from rough stones, completely empty—a symbol of God's perfection—rendered in utter visual simplicity, quite unlike the very intricate representation in the Gothic or Rococo styles.

The Mosque of Makkah

Normally, the Ka'bah is covered with a black velvet cloth which has verses from the Qur'an woven into its fabric, some of it with gold embroidery. This cover is replaced every year, and for an entire year a group of embroiderers are busy stitching, sewing, and skillfully embellishing the new drape. The Ka'bah cover used to be a gift from the Khedive of Egypt and had to be brought down from Cairo every year by a camel caravan. During pilgrimages, the cloth is pulled up lest nobody believe that this house of God is, or pretends to be, a work of art or something mysterious.

At the conclusion of the pilgrimage, the Under Secretary of the Saudi Ministry of the Interior presented me with a large piece of last year's Ka'bah cover. Muslims object to religious relics, otherwise, this one would qualify.

After undergoing a rather lax weapons check, we headed toward the mosque, brimming with holy fervor, in order to circle the Ka'bah for a total of seven times (*tawāf*). Before entering the mosque, we tried to etch into our minds the view of a particular clock tower that is only visible to people who leave at this very spot. We agreed to meet back here in two hours. It is quite clear that we would have had to be chained together in order to be able to stay together in a throng of some 40,000 pilgrims.

Journey to Makkah

With our right shoulder uncovered, we began to circle around the Ka'bah, visual center of Islam, geographical focus of a billion people's daily prayers. All the while I kept thinking that by performing the *tawāf* we are aligning ourselves with God. To the customary series of prayers, I decided to add a personal one:

Lord, make Your reality become mine!
Lord, make Your objective reality my subjective reality!

I remembered that in Muhammad's youth, this house abounded in idols, including statues of Jesus and Mary. A religious pluralism of amazing economic success! And very much in line with the current "anything goes" ideology. In those days, Makkah was a hub of international trade; nowadays, it is a center for pilgrims from all over the world. In the old days, the city would tolerate everybody for the duration of four holy months; nowadays, it tolerates only Muslims, all year long.

Among the thousands of people pushing and shoving and being pushed and shoved around, it was not easy to keep one's focus on the historic, symbolic, and spiritual power of this place and to safeguard the spirituality behind one's actions. Without that, the pilgrimage could be reduced to an exercise in physical exertion.

The Ka'bah

11

Frequently, I was jerked aside by the broad hips of Anatolian women, who were trying to hang on to their husbands' shoulders as they were forcefully strutting ahead. This was not without a comical effect, especially when the patriarch, the undaunted leader of such a formation, was forging ahead while busily reciting from a Turkish prayer book which he held high above his head. It is less funny, on the other hand, to suddenly find oneself tossed about helplessly in a heaving throng of people. This is a phenomenon well-known in soccer stadiums. The very biggest danger is, however, near the Black Stone *(Al Ḥajar Al Aswad)*. Here the newcomers are crowding in from the outside in order to start circling the Ka'bah, while those who have finished their *tawāf* are trying to push their way out. At the same time, the crowd backs up at this point, because it is customary for the pilgrim to turn to the Black Stone, raise his hands, and exclaim a "Praise the Lord!" *(al ḥamdu lillah)*.

The Black Stone is set in silver and lodged into one of the corners of the Ka'bah. Earlier I had taken an opportunity to kiss it, therefore, it did not seem right for me to mock the fascination this simple meteorite holds for the pilgrims, although it doesn't play any part in the rites of the hajj. Islam certainly abhors the worship of stones, be they black, white or gray, especially since the ancient Arabs were known for worshipping stone idols. However, there are historical as well as initiatory reasons for all the attention lavished on the Black Stone. Earlier Ka'bahs had repeatedly become victims of rainstorms, a fact that surprises no one who ever witnessed how previously dry river beds *(widyān,* sing.: *wādi)* in North Africa and the Middle East after heavy rain are turned into roaring white waters devouring everything and everybody in their path. This is how the Black Stone, which—as they say—neither hurts nor helps anybody, came to be the only surviving remainder of pre-Islamic times. It is, in a word, the Ka'bah's oldest piece!

Furthermore, it was Muhammad himself who personally installed this meteorite in its present location. When the Ka'bah was being rebuilt, Makkah's nobles were arguing over who would get the honor to return the stone to its original spot. Muhammad solved the problem by having it placed on a sheet and then asking a member of every clan to lend a hand to lift it up. As the impartial advisor, he then pushed the Stone back into the very same place it occupies today.

Those who touch this stone thus bridge the gap of time and establish as it were a physical connection with the Prophet. As a consequence, they—like billions before them—become part of a great spiritual chain (*silsilah*). This symbolic initiation, and nothing else, was all that knowledgeable fellow pilgrims and I were really interested in.

My thoughts were rudely interrupted when an unconscious woman was carried away right before my very eyes. Like all the other Malaysian women she was organized in a truly exemplary fashion, having her national colors and her personal data written on a piece of cloth affixed to the back of her head gear. This way she was easily identified. She would not have been the first woman to be crushed to death by the crowd.

Yet even among such masses, the miracle of tolerance prevails. I passed by a pilgrim who made his tireless rounds around the Ka'bah on crutches. He was probably too proud (or too poor) to have somebody push him in a wheelchair, or to be carried around in wooden contraptions by others, like thousands of other disabled people. Nobody would be so careless as to push him to the ground. Suddenly, I observed in disbelief how some fellow pilgrims proceeded to kneel down for prayers right in the middle of the moving crowd. "*Ayuha-l-hujjāj* (O you pilgrims!), why here and now?" I was about to exclaim, but then thought better of it.

In this overcrowded situation, circling seven times around the Ka'bah took me an entire hour. Fortunately, it was a relatively cool night. As little as one hour of exposure to sunlight in theses latitudes might well send the average middle-aged European to one of the Saudi clinics specializing in sunstrokes.

Having completed the *tawāf*, I quenched my thirst—in the broadest sense of the word—with waters from the legendary Zamzam fountain. I decided to bring 20 liters of its waters back to Rabat to distribute it, sip by sip, to friends and servants, as if it was worth gold. This is another way of establishing a physical, initiatory link with Makkah.

Now the time had come to say two prayer units (*rak'ah*s) near the *Maqām* of Ibrahim. The Qur'an mentions this place near the entrance of the Ka'bah as a reminder that it was originally constructed by Abraham, the ancestor of all the semites, together with Ismā'il (Ismael), the son he had from his second wife Hajar; he in turn would originate the Arab line of descent. Legend has it that Abraham once visited the Arab side of his family after having resettled them in Makkah a mere two years before because his wife,

Sarah, already much advanced in years when she became pregnant with Ishaq (Isaac), the direct ancestor of the Jewish people, no longer tolerated the other mother.

Even a number of Muslims tended to consider this both biblical as well as Qur'anic story as a benevolent piece of pious lore. They were finally convinced by the book "The Bible came from Asir", written by the Protestant professor Kamal Salibi, who with much linguistic evidence asserts that up until approximately 500 B.C., the Jewish tribes had lived in Western Arabia's Asir province between Taif and Yemen. According to the book, the legends supportive of the many rites of the pilgrimage appear to have happened exactly as narrated from generation to generation.

While looking for a place to say my prayers without much hope of succeeding, I ran into my collegue, the ambassador of Guinea in Rabat, and the Lebanese Grand Mufti. Both men had the same problem. At last we found a spot among a group of Eastern Turkmenian and Mongolian pilgrims who were resting comfortably beneath the roof of the mosque. Some were reading the Qur'an, others were chewing on something, some were sleeping in anticipation of tomorrow's call to morning prayers.

But I hurried along. In strict observance of the obligatory rites, I had to cover almost three miles as I wandered back and forth for a total of seven times between the stylized mounds of al Marwa and al Safā (sa'ī). The Qur'an refers to this place in 2:158:

> Behold! Al Safā and al Marwah are among the symbols of Allah.

We were actually walking this route in commemoration of the struggles involved in finding the original fountain of Zamzam. The records tell us how Hajar found herself in dire straits after Abraham had left her and her little son Isma'il in the valley of Makkah, which in those days had not yet been settled. Looking for water, she is said to have run back and forth between the two hills. While she frequently spotted water from above, she would lose sight of it the moment she hurried down toward it. Desperate and on the brink of exhaustion she picked up her boy, and all of a sudden the riddle was resolved: All the while Isma'il had been sitting and playing on top of the spring known today as the Zamzam fountain.

Under the conditions of the hajj, reenacting this beautiful, reassuring story of how God provides for man becomes another physical proving ground, especially since one is expected to jog over certain sections of the

14

route. The profound symbolism did not escape me, as I, thoroughly exhausted but undaunted, refreshed myself by taking a second, generous drink from the Zamzam fountain.

Finally, I had a lock cut off, took off my pilgrim's clothes, which I would not have to put on again for a few days, and concluded the first part of my hajj. Others, like my fellow pilgrims from the Senegal, inspired by asceticism, chose the more arduous variation of the hajj, which is to wear their *iḥram* clothes continuously up to the very end of their pilgrimage.

On the following day, resting up from fatigue, diarrhea, and a slight cold—unavoidable symptoms of a strenuous pilgrimage—I analyzed Saudi TV, whose entire program is essentially one continuous religious show.

Murad Hofmann in 1982

On that particular day, an imam emphasized that those who deny that Jesus was a prophet could not be considered true Muslims. He continued that blind adherence to the legal standards of earlier authorities (*taqlīd*) was also un-Islamic; nobody was dispensed from using his own abilities to reflect and reason. He followed up with quite a unique interpretation of the exclamation *"nūrun 'ala nūr!"* (Light upon Light) in the Qur'anic "Verse of the Light" (24:35). According to the imam, this means that the new "light of revelation" complements and outshines the already existing "light of reason."

After 10 years of spectacular developments in the area of architecture, urban planning, and infrastructure, Jeddah was hardly recognizable to me anymore. It became a typical American metropolis the size of Berlin. Street signs, the types of cars, billboards, gas stations—everything looked like Colorado Springs or Minneapolis. It is a strange thing to see Arabs, Sudanese, and Phillipinos populating the streets. One might easily think that one is in the New World, not the old world of Arabia.

Murad Hofmann in 1992

I spent the remaining days leading up to the decisive second part of my pilgrimage with American, Moroccan, Saudi and German friends. I was now wearing the *thawb* (in Egypt called *gallabiyyah*), the ankle-length Saudi national garb, which is elegant, loose fitting, and very convenient for praying. In this climate, the mere idea of wearing tailored suits and strangling ties is a torture.

My non-Saudi friends were mainly foreign workers, who make up about 40% of the local population. (In Dubai, they amount to approximately 90%!) It would not be the first time in Arab history if migrant workers were to take over the reigns of power. In the case of the Abbasid dynasty, this role fell to the Turkish mercenaries. This explains why migrant workers are facing a rather uncertain existence in this country, even though many of them are Muslims, too. There is no immigration policy allowing to unite families, and expulsions happen more often than not.

As early as November 12, 1762, Carsten Niebuhr arriving in Jeddah commented on the great number of "heathens from India" working in Arabia or Yemen. Like a forerunner of Amnesty International he complained that "they are not permitted to bring their wives . . . , so they prefer to return to their countries once they made their fortune."[1]

Depending on one's level of expectations, however, all of this may be easy to endure in a country where tap water, electricity, and local phone calls are free, and a liter of gasoline is cheaper than a bottle of mineral water.

A bedouin friend of mine carried me to the evening prayers in his Cadillac. We had just finished, when a pilgrim from Yemen began to raise his voice complaining loudly about how his wife had run away with pass-

---

1. Carsten Niebuhr, *Reisebeschreibungen nach Arabien und anderen umliegenden Ländern* (Zurich 1992), p. 318.

16

port and money and left him penniless. People reached for their wallets right away. The betrayed husband had availed himself of an ancient right which allows people in the mosque to speak up about their personal affairs.

The story of Abraham's willingness to sacrifice one of his sons (if He so wills!), as well as the obedient son's acquiescence in being sacrificed, has always made a strong impression on Muslims. This unconditional submission to God, demonstrated by father and son, is the central and pervasive theme in Islam. This is why the pilgrimage culminates in the emulation of this event. At the conclusion of his hajj, every pilgrim performs an animal sacrifice, symbolically reenacting the sacrifice of the ram that was substituted for Abraham's son.

It is not necessary to sacrifice an animal by one's own hand. Once, while strolling around the city, I stopped at a bank and paid 280 German Marks—about $175.00—for two sheep. I gave instructions that their meat be given to the Bosnian Muslims. On the Festival of Sacrifice, 10,000 butchers from all over the Muslim world will come together to slaughter about one million animals, including cattle, camels and my two sheep. I could rest assured that over the next few days their frozen meat would be on its way to Split.

It was evening, and I was watching the 700 ft. tall fountain in Jeddah's lagoon change its colors again and again. Today, it is the city's characteristic landmark, replacing the long since demolished, multilevel wooden houses in the old town with their characteristic covered balconies (*mushrabiyahs*). With great longing I was looking forward to the approaching high point of the hajj. "Just don't get sick before the Day of Arafat!" I told myself.

*

Together with bearing witness (*shahadah*), prayer, fasting and paying taxes (*zakah*), the pilgrimage is one of the five pillars of Islam and, as such, a must for every Muslim whose health and financial situation—after seeing to his family's and neighbors' needs—permits him to do so. The Qur'an plainly states:

> . . . pilgrimage thereto is a duty people owe to Allah - those who can afford the journey. (3:97)

No Muslim is allowed to go on a pilgrimage as long as a neighbor is in dire need! (In spite of this, in order to finance the journey many farmers in their dotage decide to sell off the land that feeds their family.)

It is not really a question of duty: the journey to Makkah is a dream come true for every Muslim, and upon returning becomes his pride and joy. When one comes back one may well find the entrance to his/her house painted green, and from this point on enjoy the ultimate prestige. There is no Ph.D., no Master's degree, no titles like "Your Excellency" or "Professor" *(ustādh)* that can possibly compete with the titulation every returning pilgrim is entitled to: Al-Hajj!"

Such a costly and potentially fatal enterprise requires painstaking spiritual and logistical preparations, even in the age of the jet plane, particularly since nowadays visas for pilgrims are subject to quotas. The fact that only one out of 1,000 eligible pilgrims is issued a visa seems to have the not quite unintended consequence of limiting the number of pilgrims from Iran to no more than 40,000. At the same time, this quota system is undermined by the indeterminable number of pilgrims from among the foreign workers in Saudi Arabia. Nothing can prevent them from heading to Makkah with a piece of cardboard for a bed and a plastic bottle of water in hand, and exploding the number of pilgrims to more than two million.

The Qur'an both admonishes and encourages the prospective pilgrim:

> And take a provision (with you) for the journey, but the best provision is right conduct. So fear Me, O people of insight. (2:197)

I read historical descriptions of the hajj dating back to the 19th century, such as Richard Burton's two-volume "Personal Narrative of a pilgrimage to Al-Madinah & Meccah" (1853) and Heinrich von Maltzahn's "Wallfahrt nach Mekka" (Pilgrimage to Makkah, 1860). Another account is the 1814 travelogue by a Swiss Muslim from a prestigious family in Basel, Ludwig Burckhardt a.k.a. Shaykh Ibrahim ibn 'Abdallah. In addition to that, I took to studying useful modern how-to books, like *Every Man's Guide to Hajj and Umrah* and *Mekka und Medina in Farbe* (Makkah and al Madinah in Color) in the series *Reisen heute* (Travel Today).

The most important preparation toward the spiritual provision for the journey was the study of the respective verses that can be found in many different places in the Qur'an, particularly in surahs 2 and 22. In addition to that, it was necessary to keep aware of the Prophet's many different com-

18

ments *(hadith)* relevant to the subject. A condensed rendition of both, Ahmad von Denffer's *Wallfahrt nach Mekkah—das Wichtigste über umra und hadsch* (Pilgrimage to Makkah—The Essential Information about 'Umrah and Hajj), München 1986, became my indispensable reference tool in solving the main problem, i.e., how to integrate the external and the inner aspects of pilgrimage.

This is not an unusual exercise for Muslims, since their faith claims every aspect of their existence, body *and* soul. In Islam, the devotion to God cannot be reduced to cerebral ruminations and a personal set of moral convictions. Praying, fasting, sacrificing and the pilgrimage require a total, absolute commitment on the part of the Muslim that goes beyond heart and mind, demanding the entire person, from top to toe. It is that—or nothing at all: This is a consequence of the Islamic principle of ontological unity *(tawhid)*.

In my hotel room in Jeddah I was passing the time leading up to the crucial days by going through my notes. Among those were the following statements by Brother Ahmad:

So, why not put it as follows: *ihrām* points to death? And *tawāf* aligns you with Allah? And *sa'i* is effort, search, and pains? And *zamzam* is life and fulfillment? And *'Arafat* lets us anticipate the Day of Resurrection? And *Muzdalifah*, darkness before the new dawn? And *Mina*, with the slaughter and the removal of the *ihrām*, a new life? And the stonings in *Mina*, the lifelong struggle against evil? But the center of life is Allah?

All rhetorical questions.

The city's loudspeakers blared the first call *(adhān)* to the afternoon prayers. Shortly before the second call *(iqāmah)*, the faithful slowly began to congregate in the hotel's tiny mosque. This time around I became the occasional *mu'adhdhin*, since it happened to be my turn to remind the group that the prayer was about to begin. I tried to follow in Bilal's footstep, the very first of a line of *mu'adhdhins* beginning 1413 lunar years before me. It was in a much weaker voice, though, that I began to exclaim in Arabic:

God alone is great! God alone is great!
I declare there is no other god but Allah!
I declare that Muhammad is Allah's messenger!
Come to the prayer! Come to your well-being!
The prayer is about to begin! The prayer is about to begin!

God alone is great! God alone is Great!
There is no other God but Allah!

We asked a very dark-skinned man from the Maldives to lead us in prayer as our imam, and we didn't have to ask twice.

In the course of our dinner together I noticed that nobody seemed to have an ounce of appetite. This was due to the excitement that tomorrow, on the 8th day of the month of pilgrimage, we were to move from Jeddah via Makkah to Minah, which would serve as a kind of base camp for the most significant days of our hajj. We could not sleep all night long, and at five o'clock in the morning, much too early, most of us showed up in the lobby, wearing their pilgrims' clothes again.

We stopped briefly in Makkah in order to circumambulate the Ka'bah one more time *(tawāf al qudūm)*, this time under the scorching sun. Just like many other pilgrims, I tried to protect myself with an umbrella, but this proved utterly impossible lest you risk gouging out someone's eye, or losing your own.

In the yard of the huge mosque, on the level of the Ka'bah, everything became completely gridlocked, so I escaped up to the first story of the shaded gallery. In return I had to put up with a wider radius. Circling the Ka'bah seven times up there meant covering a distance of 3.5 miles, and that in 110 °F heat. No pity, please! By all means, avoid feeling sorry for yourself! If his focus is right, to a pilgrim everything comes easy. Someone who was walking by my side even covered the entire distance with his little son on his shoulders!

The view from first story was absolutely mesmerizing and of striking aesthetic power. The Ka'bah appears like the motionless center of a giant disc in a slow and silent counterclockwise revolution. The scene changes only at prayer times: At this point, the Ka'bah becomes the center of concentric circles made up of 40,000 or more shining white bodies who want the same, seek the same, do the same—and thus come to symbolize total submission on a global scale.

Multistoried structures circumscribe the inner court of the mosque, with the Ka'bah at dead center. Everything is dominated by sumptuous, sometimes green marble. Seven gigantic minarets in Indo-Islamic style are the connecting elements that hold the Ka'bah in its setting like a precious gem. I had to tear myself away—or miss the bus altogether.

After 45 minutes on the bus we finally arrived in the city of Mina, which is only a little more than 3 miles from Makkah. Mina was going to be our jumping-off point for the Day of 'Arafah. And what lets us know what the Day of 'Arafah is all about? Hajj is 'Arafah, so says the Prophet, and 'Arafah is hajj.

This year (1992 A.C./1412 A.H.), June 19 is the 9th day of the month of the pilgrimage, the Day of 'Arafah.

There are only a few parallel roadways connecting Mina or Makkah to 'Arafah, and more than two million pilgrims are transported over a distance of about 6 to 10 miles on as much as 50,000 buses. They both cause and suffer a truly awesome, unprecedented traffic chaos that could easily qualify for the Guiness' Book of Records.

Some are trying to walk. But given the temperature prevailing as early as 8 o'clock this is no option. At that very moment I notice a man dropping to the ground as he was trying to carry his father piggy-back—circulatory collapse.

When we finally arrived in the tent city erected around the Mount of 'Arafah, the air was glimmering with heat—120°F in the shade, which makes it considerably more than 130°F in the sun! And not a whiff of a breeze in the air. The sun's impact is relentless: Breathing is very difficult, and every movement is a chore. As I found out pretty soon, German feet are susceptible to burning within just a few minutes while waiting in line in front of the toilet. During the hottest time of the day, I sought refuge in a small tent which I shared with a professor of economic statistics from Georgetown University in Washington. The neighboring tent belonged to none other than Shaykh Mahfoud Naḥnaḥ from Algiers.

It became a long and wonderful day of contemplation, reflection, of prayers, and invaluable conversations. Never since my boyhood days, during Jesuit retreat exercises had I possessed this inner certainty of a clear spiritual focus on God. The Day of 'Arafah is nothing but dialogue with Him. Such is the embodiment of our constant cry: Here I stand before you, our God!—*Labbayka, Allahuma, labbayk!*

This, therefore, is the meaning of "tarrying" (*wuqūf*) before God on the plane of 'Arafah. Millions of people, wrapped in burial shrouds, leave everything behind on this day, exist only for God, embrace their mortality, and go on pleading and praying with a degree of fervor and confidence never achieved before—and hardly ever after. It was here, on his "farewell pilgrimage" shortly before his death in 632, that Muhammad delivered a sermon which is recited year after year, on the same day, the very same place, in exactly the self-same words. Back then, he had admonished the Muslims: "Treat women in a manner respectful of God!" and had concluded with this question:

I leave for you the Book of God. If you abide by it, you shall never go wrong. And on the Day of Judgment you will be asked about me. Tell me, what will you answer?

It is said that the people who were present responded:

We will bear witness that you delivered the message, discharged your duties as a prophet and gave wise and sincere counsel.

I bear witness, too, and I do so today with 2.2 million men and women from all over the world.

It is the custom to stay in 'Arafah until just after sunset, only to hurry off down the 4.5 mile stretch toward Muzdalifah. There was such a rush and confusion that the professor and I had lost our bus. Wandering around among hundreds of buses, we were looking for seats.

Suddenly, I noticed somebody waving me to approach him. It was a friend of mine, Muhammad Azmani, Morocco's Minister of Industry and Trade. To run into him, in a crowd of two million people! (Another "accident" that confirmed my conviction that there is no such thing as a genuine accident in God's world.) That is how, at a time of crisis, I became a temporary, unofficial member of the official Moroccan hajj delegation.

First this tremendous rush, and now we found ourselves sitting on the stranded bus for a total of three hours, drenched in sweat, before it was able to crawl forward for all but three yards. As usual, all the pilgrims must try to get to the same place at the same time. The traffic police attempted to intervene, but only succeeded in worsening the chaos. A few pilgrims were trying to take the direct route on foot, across the dark volcanic mountains, their forms contrasting off of the black rocks like lost and lonely white ghosts.

Caught in stop-and-go traffic, we did not reach the city of Muzdalifah—close but yet so far—until 11 P.M. Lead by an imam from Rabat, we were holding our evening and night prayers together, our sore knees resting on just those tiny but sharp pieces of gravel, the size of chick-peas, from which we were to pick up 49 pebbles in order to be appropriately supplied for the rites of stoning (*rajm*), that were to take place on the following days.

We were also promised some food, but we had to be on our way before it could get to us. I didn't really regret this. Over the past days of the hajj, I had gotten used to make do with some pieces of chicken, a few peas, an apple, and a banana. But drinking was foremost on our mind. Luckily there was never a lack of water. Throughout the pilgrimage, the government authorities are distributing 80 million plastic bags, each holding slightly over a quart of water. At every major intersection in Mina small cartons of fruit juice were thrown into the crowd. Because of that I never had to touch my emergency stash of Coca Cola after all.

At about two o'clock in the morning our bus returned to Mina and stopped near one of the three pillars that were to be stoned. The intention was to symbolize the final rejection of evil in oneself and also in the world around us. (A purpose which corresponds somewhat to the Catholic sacrament of confirmation.) I pushed my way in close enough to hit the pillar with my pebbles (traditionally flinging them with two fingers only), yet also maintained a safe distance to avoid getting caught in a hail of stones from behind.

A truly touchy situation! Many simple minded people can easily get carried away by the idea that at least once in a lifetime they are able to open fire on Satan. Therefore, the odd good size chunk of rock may be zipping by, with sandals and even umbrellas following in its wake.

A group of little boys armed with scissors waited in front of our bus. Didn't I say so? Since we did not opt for shaving our heads, they at least wanted to cut off a lock for the sum of three riyals, as it finally happened.

After that, having fulfilled all our hajj obligations, we could have left the status of *ihram* and with it stopped wearing our pilgrim's attire. Instead, we found ourselves so elated that we were swept along in a kind of pious rapture. So before dawn we decided to hurry on to Makkah. There was no need to talk our bleary-eyed Phillipino bus driver into it—he was wearing the pilgrim's cloth himself.

Now we had to walk around the Ka'bah for a third time, this time in the cover of night (*tawāf al ifādah*). At least 200,000 other pilgrims seemed, however, to have had the same brilliant idea and unaccountable energy reserves. Thus the pushing and shoving was even worse than last time. As a result, the seven-fold circumambulation of "The House," followed by the jogging and walking back-and-forth between al Safā and al Marwah, also for seven times, altogether took me a total of two exhausting hours.

It was 4:30 in the morning on the Day of Sacrifice, the 10th day of the month of pilgrimage, and we had to muster our last ounce of strength and composure in order to join 800,000 other believers for the morning prayers in the Great Mosque of Makkah, almost in a trance.

The quality of their voices, together with the perfection of their recitation distinguish the *mu'adhdhin*s and the imams in the *haram* of Makkah as the *"crème de la crème"*. Their chanting builds into a magnificent incantation of sublime artistic quality. In fact, their recitation of the Qu'ran reaches the level of acoustic meditation. Quite in contrast to the Maliki school in North Africa, the Hanbali school in Saudi Arabia fortunately permits more aestheticized forms of prayer which are apt to transport even bleary-eyed pilgrims like myself into a world that knows no weariness.

Shortly after six A.M., we had finally made it back to our guest house in Mina. After being up and about for 26 hours, we felt emotionally and physically drained. My fellow pilgrims and I embraced each other, exclaiming *"Hajj mubārak! Hajj maqbūl!"* (May your hajj be blessed and accepted [by God].) Shaykh Naḥnaḥ was sobbing, delighted with my new status.

After that, I took off my pilgrim's attire for good—for this time anyway. With a sore throat, but full of happiness, I sank into my bed, thanked God for letting me terminate my pilgrimage and pleaded with Him to accept it. The incredibly noisy rattling of the air conditioner did not disturb my deep slumber in the least. Those of us who were exhausted sought to regenerate ourselves during the Festival of Sacrifice *('Id al aḍhā)*, while the more resilient pilgrims were busy slaughtering their animals on the spot. The person who performs the sacrifice is permitted to consume a small part of the meat himself, the rest is given away to needy people, not necessarily pilgrims. Some skeletons are hung up to dry in the sun, sometimes on the outside of pick-up trucks. One can easily imagine the stench that spreads. Then again—one can't.

That day I was worried about my next door neighbor from Washington and repeatedly knocked on his door. I had a feeling that he had pushed himself too far. Indeed, he had to ask me to take his remaining pebbles and fill in for him for the last two rounds of ritual stoning. This is permissible, because it is quite possible to perform the entire hajj in lieu of someone who is unable to go through it himself.

Journey to Makkah

*

On the second day of the Festival of Sacrifice, together with 150 pilgrims from around the world, among them the Sultan of Brunei and a son of the Iranian Prime Minister Rafsandjani, I was a guest of King Fahd b. Abdelaziz at his palace in Mina. (By the way, the Saudi monarch had invited—not just for lunch but for the entire hajj—13,000 Muslims from the former Soviet Union). In the course of the royal reception, I found myself sitting between the highly successful Egyptian author Anis Mansour and Muhammad Afzat Zullah, Chief Justice of Pakistan. He told me that he had never upheld a verdict sentencing a thief to have his hand cut off. Since monarchs are wont to keep people waiting, we had a lot of time to talk about Islam, Islam, and Islam, as people do whose hearts are full of it. The pilgrimage is both a summit conference as well as a huge international grass-roots meeting of Muslims.

King Fahd is protected by scowling bodyguards dressed in traditional uniforms, who most likely already served his father, the legendary Abd al-Aziz Ibn Saud (died 1953). However, beyond scimitar and pistol, they are also armed with machine pistols.

In the course of my conversation with the king I noticed that he knew quite a lot about me. It had been suggested to him that inviting me would send a signal in view of the malicious media campaign in Germany, waged against me at that time in my capacity as a Muslim.

The meal proceeded in accordance with Arabo-Islamic etiquette as prescribed by the Qur'an (see "At the table with Muslims"). Every course and dish is served all at once, with table bending oppulence, and all food is placed within everybody's easy reach. Once seated, people talk very little, eat fast, and bid farewell as soon as they are full. Surah 33 explains:

... And when you have taken your meal, disperse, without engaging in conversation. (33:53)

For this reason, the king is always the last to remain at the table.

On that evening, Minister Azmani and I were elbowing our way through the crowded, smelly streets of Mina to carry out the second stoning. Like the police officers around us, we covered nose and mouth with a handkerchief soaked in Eau de Cologne. We were running an ecological gauntlet: past trash festering in the sun, pilgrims camping out on the asphalt, and cars with engines constantly running to operate the air conditioner. These asphalt-pilgrims, migrant workers without guidance of a *mutawwif*, were leading an illegal, albeit quite tangible existence. On this day, a woman from Indonesia even gave birth to a little girl on her cardboard mat.

On the third (and last) day of the Festival of Sacrifice (June 13), I went right after the morning prayer and all by myself, to discharge my duty of ritual stoning, for myself as well as my neighbor. In the streets, the first pilgrims were just beginning to rise from their makeshift beds. The small amounts of personal water reserves they carried were first and foremost used for the ritual washing (see "Five Times a Day—as Directed"). Even some street vendors were already up and about. Combining hajj with commerce has always been permissible. Many pilgrims are earning their trip back home by selling off whatever they brought from their native countries: ivory trinkets, silver jewelry, or fabrics.

An Anatolian farmer crossed my path and asked rather casually: "*Seytan nerede?*" (Where is the devil?), as if he expected everybody to know this and speak Turkish to boot. With a dead pan face I gave the correct directions—in Turkish—for him to find the third pillar, the one scheduled for stoning that day. Never before had I been able to locate the devil with such a degree of precision.

The next day we returned to Jeddah by way of Makkah where we performed the farewell *tawāf* (*tawāf al wadāʿ*). Since we arrived in time for the afternoon prayer, the mosque was bursting at the seams. This time, I circled the Kaʿbah on the rooftop of the surrounding gallery, although my feet were able to touch the hot surface for but a few seconds at a time. I felt like the proverbial bear trained to dance on a heated plate.

But then I decided so sit on the gallery for quite some time, eagerly soaking in the view of this incredibly beautiful mosque so that it would stay with me for a long time. I felt homesick for Makkah even before having left.

When checking in for the return flight to Casablanca, I handed back my pilgrim's ID-card. The offical seemed to be relieved at any pilgrim leaving the country voluntarily. The jumbo jet headed straight for Tunis, so at least on this flight it was clear in which way to turn for prayers. In fact, turning their backs to the cockpit, the stewards prayed in the aisle. For inflight reading I chose TIME magazine dated June 15. The cover showed a mosque. It ran a feature entitled "Islam—Should the World Be Afraid?"

A PHILOSOPHICAL
APPROACH TO ISLAM

On September 8, 1980, I drove up to Venusberg Hill in Bonn, site of the diplomatic training school of the German Foreign Office, to participate in a seminar on Islam. At that time, I had no idea that only two years later I would find myself as a pilgrim in Makkah. The magnitude of the turning point I was about to face in my life did not begin to dawn upon me until I had a chance to reflect on the astute lecture by my Muslim collegue, Muhammad Ahmad Hobohm, and got into a conversation with another speaker, Imam Muhammad Ahmad Rassoul, the German-Egyptian head of an Islamic publishing house in Cologne.

I showed him a 12 page manuscript I had been fine tuning for quite some time. In view of my son's upcoming 18th birthday, I had drafted it to record for him the (few) things I considered unquestionably true—from a philosophical point of view.

Rassoul's reaction was astonishing: If I really was convinced of what I had written down , then I was a Muslim! At first, I hesitated to believe him, but he subsequently convinced me when he asked for the rights to publish my paper as "A Philosophical Approach to Islam."[2]

A few days later, on Sept. 25, 1980, I professed my faith: "I bear witness that there is no divinity besides Allah, and I bear witness that Muhammad is Allah's messenger."

---

2.   Murad W. Hoffmann, *Ein philosophischer Weg zum Islam*, 3rd edition (Munich 1997). English version, *A Philosophical Approach to Islam* (Cologne 1983).

*

Trying to give an account of one's spiritual growth—leading up to such a crucial step—is a rather questionable enterprise. Hermann Hesse had it right in his 1919 novella *Klein and Wagner*: "To verbalize it virtually guarantees that everything is misunderstood, found trite, and tedious." In his novel *Das Glasperlenspiel,* he sounded a similar warning against any attempt to put meaningful internal experiences into words: " . . . be respectful of what is 'meaningful,' but don't assume it could be taught," says his master musician.[3]

Besides, many a greater mind has failed in this attempt. Tempestuous Omar, later to be the 2nd Caliph, had been violently persecuting the Muslims up until his sudden conversion. It is impossible to fathom why, in the midst of a family feud, he was won over by Islam upon reading the 20th surah *(Ta Ha).*[4] Abu Hamid al Ghazali, the outstanding mystic rationalist of the 11/12th century correctly states in his confessions *(Al Munqidh min al Dalal)* that he did not internalize the articles of faith because of any particular documented proof, but that they became enshrined in his soul by "myriads of deep-rooted causes, attendant circumstances and experiences whose details cannot possibly be recounted." In the final analysis, his "return back to Islam" came as the result of a "light" which God cast into his soul.[5] The same is true for the fascinating book about Muhammad Asad's *Road to Makkah,* where the experience of conversion is mentioned in but a few scant lines which also are not very illuminating to the skeptical reader. In one passage he even claims to have soaked up Islam as if it were by osmosis.[6] A similar thing obviously happened to Christian (Abdul-Hadi) Hoffmann during his instant conversion, which "struck out of the blue!"[7]

I, too, had felt Islam's magnetic attraction for many years, if not decades, because I felt intellectually and emotionally so much at home with Islam as if I had been there before. At the same time, on my road there I had three

---

3.   Hermann Hesse, *Wege nach Innen* (Frankfurt 1973), and *Das Glasperlenspiel* (1943), several editions available from Suhrkamp Verlag.
4.   Sahih al Bukhari, *The Early Years of Islam,* trans. Muhammad Asad (Gibraltar 1981).
5.   Al Ghazali, *Faith and Practice of al-Ghazali* (London 1953), p. 75.
6.   Muhammad Asad, *The Road to Makkah* (Gibraltar 1982).
7.   Christian H. Hoffmann, *Zwischen allen Stühlen* (Bonn 1995), p. 25.

Murad Hofmann with Muhammad Asad and Hamida Asad in 1985

key experiences which were of a human, aesthetic, and philosophical nature.

*

It is rather strange how the first key experience is tied to Algiers.

In 1960, I had spent two months in Château-neuf-sur-Loire preparing for the entrance exam to a senior German foreign service career. I had to bring my French proficiency up to speed. Everyday I would read detailed reports in the French press about the war of independence in Algeria. As part of the entrance exam we were required to deliver a five minute lecture on a subject that was assigned by lottery drawing barely 10 minutes earlier. My topic, "The Algerian Question," almost ruined my chances, not because I new too little, but because I knew too much about it.

A few months later, as I was getting ready to leave for my job as Attaché in Geneva, my training councilor casually mentioned over a bowl of salad that my assignment had just been changed—to Algiers.

In 1961/62, I found myself there in the middle of extremely bitter and bloody guerilla warfare between the French troops and the National

Liberation Front (*Front de Libération National/F.L.N.*) which had been going on for eight years. While I was there, the so-called *Organisation Armée Secrète* (O.A.S.), an ultra-conservative French terrorist organization made up of rebel soldiers as well as French and Spanish settlers, had joined the fray.

Each day dozens of people were killed in the streets of Algiers, mostly from close range, execution style, simply for being an Arab, or for speaking up for Algeria's independence. Whenever I heard the rattling of an automatic gun, I would phone home to send my American wife on a quick shopping errand, because experience had taught us that there was a good 20 minutes lag time between assassinations.

My foremost responsibility was looking after Germans who had deserted from the French Foreign Legion, and getting them back home—absurd as it may sound—with the help of the French authorities. Ever since the year before, when the entire 1st. Paratrooper Regiment of the Legion had deserted, there were hundreds of these poor (but romantic) devils around. What an affinity to death they had! Many were recruited by the O.A.S. as "commandos" and thus ended up in the crossfire. Sometimes, in the name of the Federal Republic of Germany, I had to place carnations on the graves of assassinated ex-legionaires who, shortly after their honorable or not so honorable discharge from the Legion, had taken up veritable kamikaze-jobs as guardians on isolated farms.

Every time I had to visit Mustafa Hospital to sort out the Germans from among the injured deposited in the hallway, I carried my Walther gun on my belt—loaded, cocked, with the safety "off" for a fast draw. I did not make eye contact when somebody walked in my direction, but instead watched people's hands. On passing each other by, men would turn around and walk backwards for a few steps—just to be on the safe side. My wife was so concerned about my safety that she sometimes insisted on accompanying me. She would guard my back by walking a few steps behind me, a razor-sharp camping knife up her sleeve.

Algeria left memories that still haunt me, even today. On my way to the France V radio station, where I was scheduled to give an innocuous interview about the "situation of stage dancing in the Federal Republic of Germany," my VW Bug's gas pump suddenly quit on me in a narrow, steeply declining serpentine of the upper *rue d'Isly*. A line of honking cars began to back up behind me. Both sides of the street were blocked by parked cars, so I had no choice but to move on, coasting downhill, with my foot always on the brake. An Arab who was crossing the street in front of me was suddenly shot from the walkway by a European looking gunman and collapsed right in front of my left front fender. With his gun, the assassin motioned me to drive on so that he could finish off his victim. But I would not and could not possibly do that. Finally, he condescended to walk around and give his victim the *coup de grâce*. After that he slowly walked away, without the least sign of haste.

I was equally outraged when I once stood by helplessly to watch O.A.S. operatives ignite a car filled with gasoline canisters and push it down an embankment straight into an Arab section of the city. As an undesirable witness to such situations one might end up on somebody's hit-list. My barber in El-Biar was well aware of that. When one day O.A.S. commandos attacked and destroyed the telegraph office across from his shop on Boulevard Galiéni, he just swiveled my chair around.

His reaction was not any more bizarre than the diversionary tactic of the police officer who, in May 1962, offered to guard my car, parked near El Biar library, while it was being consumed by fire, without anybody intervening.

On March 18, 1962, in Evian, French president Charles de Gaulle and the provisional government of the F.L.N. agreed on a cease-fire and scheduled the independence of Algeria for July of the same year. At that point, the O.A.S. escalated their terror in order to provoke the Algerians into breaking the agreement. Now they began to execute systematically the young Algerian academics, and even shot women for simply wearing the Islamic dress. In the last days before independence, they shot the very last Algerian street vendor in El-Biar right under my office window.

The French neighbors in my street threw everything out of their windows that could have been of use to the victors. But the refrigerators landed on soft heaps of kitchen waste; there had not been any trash pickup for weeks (to the rats' delight).

Deplorable events such as these informed my first intimate encounter with living Islam. I witnessed the patience and resilience of the Algerian people in the face of extreme suffering, their overwhelming discipline during Ramaḍan, their confidence of victory, as well as their humanity amidst such misery, and I felt that their religion played a major role in all that.

Their humanity made its biggest impression on me when my wife suffered a miscarriage in the emotional wake of those tragedies, euphemistically called *"événements"* (happenings). The bleeding started in the middle of the night. But because of the strict curfew all night (shooting without warning!), no ambulance dared to pick us up until 6 A.M. When the time had finally arrived, I noticed that the ambulance was unable to find our street, because on this very night O.A.S. people had painted over every street sign. All of the alleys in my block were now called either "rue Salan", "rue Jouhaud"—after generals in opposition to de Gaulle—or "rue O.A.S."

After a long delay we were finally on our way to Professor Schamoun's clinic (shortly before the O.A.S. blew it up). However, upon reaching the valley called Les Femmes Sauvages, we ran into a roadblock set up by the tough *Compagnie Républicaine de Sécurité* (C.R.S). Although he was sounding his siren, our driver was only making painfully slow progress. My wife, feeling that she was about to loose consciousness, made me memorize her rare blood group, just in case. It was zero—negative.

Upon hearing this, the Algerian driver turned around and offered himself as a donor for this particular blood type. He, the Arab Muslim, in the middle of the war, was going to do this for an infidel foreigner.

In order to find out what makes those incredible "natives" tick, I began to read "their book," the Qur'an, in the French translation by Pesle/Tidjani. I have never stopped reading it, to this very day.

So far I had encountered the Qur'an only through the open windows of Qur'anic schools in the southern Algerian M'Zab region, recited by Berber children in a language foreign to them. This was something I had always scoffed at. I had not realized until much later that since the Qur'an is God's own revealed word, its literal recitation is justified under any circumstance. I also had a rather uncomfortable encounter with an Algerian in the bar of the Hotel Transméditerranée in Ghardaia. He responded angrily when I told him that I was reading the Qur'an. Evidently, he objected strongly even to the very existence of translations. To him, the attempt to translate the word of God from Arabic into any other language was sheer blasphemy. In this respect, too, it took me a while to comprehend his reaction. Arabic can make temporally indeterminate statements. References about future events that are certain to happen can be expressed in the past tense since in God's view they are as good as having taken place. Furthermore, Arabs like to insinuate things without spelling them out. Apart from that, we have the familiar problem that words for the same concept in two languages rarely mean the exact same thing, and don't convey the same associations and emotions. That is why every Qur'an translation unavoidably is a reductionist interpretation, bound to impoverish the original semanticly. The man at the bar was right!

Algeria, the country that gave me so much, was going to be my destiny never to let go. In 1966, when diplomatic relations were interrupted, Switzerland became the country protecting German interests in Algeria. At that time I happened to be working at the German embassy in Berne. Of course, I was considered to be the ideal liaison to the Swiss Foreign Office, assuring a line of communication to our skeleton crew in Algiers. Week after week, Bonn's diplomatic pouch to Algeria first landed on my desk. In 1987, 25 years after my first posting there, I returned to Algeria as ambassador. Even after I had been accredited to neighboring Morocco in 1990, I could never quite completely stop thinking about this still tragic, still suffering Algeria. Can this be mere coincidence?

*

The second key experience that led me to Islam was Islamic art—and thereby hangs a tale. I am a veritable "beauty freak," and from a very young age I had been an admirer of formal beauty and always sought to get to the heart of it, even as my American mother-in-law continuously admonished me in the traditional puritanical way that beauty was only "skin-deep"— nothing but a superficial illusion.

In 1951, when I received one of the generous scholarships for "exceptionally talented" students granted by the Bavarian Ministry of Culture, I went right out and spent the entire first amount on a life-size Hanfstaengl-reproduction of "Girl with the Mango Fruits" by Paul Gauguin. Unlike most students, I was not holed up barrack-style in the dormitories of the prestigeous Maximilaneum building on the other side of the Isar river. Rather, I analyzed my Gauguin in the "Wohnheimsiedlung am Maßmannplatz," a Bauhaus indebted housing center with a social-revolutionary flavor. There, like nowhere else, both students and blue-collar workers shared rooms. Soon I was convinced that the static arts, such as painting, sculpture, architecture, calligraphy, and other similar forms owe

33

their aesthetic impact to the illusion of motion, so to speak *frozen motion*, a principle derived from dancing. Representational art becomes the more beautiful to us the more it becomes kinetic—sophisticated at projecting dynamics.

This is how I became fascinated with dance, an obsession—"balletomania"—which drove me into every ballet evening at Munich's Prinzregententheater. From that point on, my interest in every facet of dance began to escalate. Every free hour between appearances in the court room I spent in ballet studios near the Palace of Justice. I obtained a home ballet bar in order to learn at least some of the fundamentals of classical dance and to know more intimately what I was more and more writing about. Not everybody appreciates that this ethereal form of art is the result of extremely hard physical work. Only through trying myself in due course I learnt, for instance, to recognize an *"entrechat huit"* jump, and to distinguish the technique of suggesting floatation in mid-air (*ballon*) from a really high jump (*élévation*).[8]

My favorite was a private studio run by the former Russian émigré ballerina Lula of Sachnowsky, who produced graduates the likes of Angle Albrecht. In the mid-fifties, this school would grow into "Les Ballets Sachnowsky, a small company which, somewhat pretentiously, performed not only in the city of Munich, but also ventured to small provincial towns throughout the backwaters of Southern Bavaria. I was in charge of contracts, public relations, lighting, as well as supervising the even application of make-up based on clear visibility from the 7th row. In 1955, Karl Viktor Prince zu Wied and I founded the nonprofit "Friends of the Ballet" society in Munich, and the two of us took over the dance reviews section of "Die Abendzeitung," a tabloid Munich evening paper.

What followed next can be summed up quickly. As expert ballet critic for "Das Tanzarchiv" (Cologne), "Ballet Today" (London), and "Dance News" (New York) from 1954 to 1980, and also as an Instructor for History of Dance and Ballet Aesthetics at the Cologne Stage Dance Institute from 1971 to 1973, I became acquainted with ballet studios and dance theaters all over the world. I would occasionally slip into the role of an impresario

---

8.   If interested in the steps and the terminology of Classical Ballet, consult A. J. Waganowa, *The Fundamentals of Classical Ballet* (translated from the Russian by Jochen Scheibe) (Berlin 1964); also Muriel Stuart and George Balanchine, *The Classic Ballet* (New York 1952).

Margot Fonteyn on the left and Dr. Hofmann on the right, ca. 1957

to bring Margot Fonteyn, Beryl Grey, or George Balanchine to Germany, while also bombarding German Ministers of Culture with studies and memos calling for the establishment of a German national ballet company. I spent several vacations in New York to track down faded and forgotten stars that had once made dance history—great people like Ted Shawn at Jacob's Pillow, Paul Swan, and legendary women like Hanya Holm and Martha Graham, and questioning these historical witnesses about even earlier legends like Isidora Duncan, Anna Pavlova, Vaslav Nijinski, or Serge Diaghileff.

Many of my friends and acquaintances in the world of dance had actually no idea that lawyering and later diplomacy were my day jobs. Others suspected that the true object of my obsession was not beauty, but the beauties. Admittedly, women with names like Bambi or Judy had been entering my world of late, and being beautiful was part of their jobs as fashion models, centerfolds, or dancers. Eroticism, after all, does have its legitimate place. But my true bible remained Gilbert's and Kuhn's *A History of Aesthetics*.[9] As an aficionado of ballet—an entirely nonrepresentational,

---

9.   Katherine Gilbert and Helmut Kuhn, *A History of Aesthetics* (Bloomington, Indiana 1953).

abstract art that gives form to music—I was honestly trying to discover and lay bare the causes that compel us to perceive certain objects or movements as beautiful.[10] In order to nail down the fundamentals of the aesthetics of movement, I buried myself for weeks in the Bavarian Forest above the hamlet of Drachselsried. There it began to dawn upon me that as humans, we have no choice but to perceive as beautiful the healthy human body and everything that emulates its proportions; that we are obsessive visual analysts who are trying to break down the chaotic plurality of the world into simplified, archaic and archetypical forms and patterns that are easily digestible for us optically. Furthermore, I found that we visually process pictures in the same direction as we are writing—as Europeans from left to right, as Arabs from right to left. I realized hat movement —since it can signal danger—instinctively monopolizes our attention. Finally, I understood that centrifugal movements—in contrast to centripedal ones—appeal to us because our minds project these liberally into infinity.[11]

At the end of this road, Islamic art became a powerful and exhilarating key experience for me. Was it not the static equivalent of the very qualities that had made good ballet choreography so appealing to me: the high degree of abstraction, the human dimensions, the inner dynamics, the reach towards infinity—and all of that embedded in a spirituality unique to Islam?

Major architectural feats like the Alhambra in Granada and the Great Mosque in Cordoba convinced me at first sight that they are true products of a sublime culture in its prime. I could very well understand what Rainer Maria Rilke felt after visiting the Cordoba mosque, crudely converted into a "cathedral":

> ever since Cordoba, I am full of rabid anti-Christian sentiments. I am reading the Qur'an, and at times it assumes a voice in which I feel, ever so powerful, like the wind in the flute of the organ.[12]

---

10. Wilfried Hofmann, "Of Beauty and the Dance: Towards an Aaesthetics of Ballet," *Dance Perspectives*, New York 1973, no. 55. German original: "Von der Schönheit im Tanz - Zu den Grundlagen der Ballettästhetik," *Das Tanzarchiv*, Cologne 1973/1974, Nr. 6-8.

11. Hofmann, *A Philosophical Approach to Islam*.

12. Quoted by Eva Perkuhn in: *Die Theorie zum arabischen Einfluß auf die europäische Musik des Mittelalters* (Alldorf 1976), p. 110.

From that point on, Islamic art took the place of classical ballet and became my new aesthetic home. Art from the ancient world, Romanesque and Gothic styles, Renaissance, Rococo and Bauhaus, I would intellectually appreciate as accomplished, original, interesting or even ingenious—but it never resonated with me emotionally.

In the meantime, surrounded at home by abstract or Islamic art, I understand the appeal of this religion's art form much better. Even so, western art history still has a hard time even defining Islamic art.

Its secret seems to lie in the intimate and universal presence of Islam as a religion in all of its artistic manifestations: Calligraphy, space filling arabesque ornaments, carpet patterns, mosque and housing architecture, as well as urban planning. I am thinking of the brightness of the mosques which banishes any mysticism, of the democratic spirit of their architectural layout; I am also thinking of the introspective quality of Muslim palaces, their anticipation of paradise in gardens full of shade, fountains and rivulets; of the intricate socially functional structure of old Islamic urban centers (*madinah*s), which fosters community spirit and transparency of the market, tempers heat and wind, and assures the integration of the mosque and adjacent welfare centers for the poor, schools and hostels into the market and living quarters.

People who are familiar with *suq*s (markets) like the ones in Damascus, Istanbul, Cairo, Tunis or Fez, know them all. Big or small, they are all well-integrated Islamic organisms functioning much along the same lines. Many a time I would stroll through the suq of Rabat's sister city, Salé, in order to regenerate myself on its *genius loci*. It is a kind of social biotope, where everybody—whether young or old, healthy or crippled, rich or poor, white or black—has his place; where there is neither rush nor time pressure, no cheating the customer, no alcohol, no motor traffic, no tourists, no thievery, and no extremism. Everything here seems measured, solidly based on time-tested traditions. Here, where every purchase comes with a little chat, stores close during prayers.

What I experienced as so blissfully Islamic in so many places—in Lisbon's Islamic Gulbenkian-Museum, in the Umayad Mosque in Damascus, in Cairo's Ibn Tulun, the ancient mosque of Qayrawān or the Salimiyah in Ederne—is the tangible effect which Islamic harmony, the Islamic way of life, and the Islamic treatment of space leave on both heart and mind.

*

Before embarking on the particular philosophical road that would definitely lead me to Islam and bring about a third key experience, I spent my teenage-years in Jesuit instruction as a Prefect of a rather militant Catholic youth organization, the Congregatio Mariana (MC). Strong romantic ties to that movement had been forged during the NS-Regime, when our teenage underground resistance group was one of the lucky few which neither the Gestapo nor the SD, the Nazi intelligence service were able to crack. Not even my absent-minded father, a typical professor of mathematics, was allowed to be aware of my participation. Every week, under utmost precautions, we met a Jesuit priest in a crypt. Everybody only knew his own group. As time went on, we gradually managed to recruit for our group the best and most popular students from all of the high schools in town, and thus managed to subvert the local Hitler Youth organization. After the war, when we surfaced, we were surprised at the sheer size of our congregation: over 80 boys! And did we ever relish being able to pursue whatever had been in style for romantic young people since the Twenties: hiking, camping, singing strumming the guitar, and traveling to Rome for the "Holy Year."

As an insider I was intimately familiar with Catholic faith and society and naturally expected to join the Jesuit Society of Jesus (S.J.). Yet even back then I began to ask myself the same question that Carl Jacob Burkhardt had posed, namely, whether a theologian can possibly be a Christian.[13] It began to bother me more and more that the Christian revelation should be understood *a priori* according to the extreme interpretation given to it by Paul, the belated apostle.[14]

Despite my extensive flirts with Ludwig Wittgenstein's philosophy and an epistemology whose radicalism has the whiff of agnosticism about it, I was always clear in my mind that there is no proof for the *non*-existence of God. Equally unimpressed by the utilitarian attitude of Pascal's famous wager, I continued to maintain with Richard Swinburn that it is extremely unlikely that God does not exist.[15]

---

13. Hugo von Hofmannsthal and Carl J.Burckhardt, *Briefwechsel* (Frankfurt 1957), letter dated January 15, 1929.
14. Ibid., letter dated January 12, 1929.
15. Richard Swinburn, *The Existence of God* (Oxford 1979).

Statistical probabilities are of course as inadequate for scientifically proving the existence of God as are ontological and causal arguments, which have been shown to be utterly self-deceptive. We cannot speculate as we might have done before Kant. Therefore, the intellectual acceptance or denial of God always remains a matter of faith, which in the final analysis is contingent on whatever seems *plausible* to the individual person.

As soon as I had made an affirmative decision in the matter of faith, I was faced with questions concerning the nature of communication between God and man. I was convinced not only of the possibility, but the necessity of divine interference, since the histories of man, science, and the law demonstrate beyond the shadow of a doubt, that the mere empirical study of nature does not enable us to find the correct relationship to the world around us, God, and ourselves. Are scientific discoveries not notoriously prone to obsolescence? Just witness the amusing history of economic theory, the "law of nature," and physics.

Embracing both the possibility and necessity of revelation, I was faced with yet another decision in matters of faith: Whose authenticity to accept or reject, the Judeo-Christian, or the Islamic prophecy?

The answer to this question grew out of my third key experience. It happened when I came across a verse which is repeated several times in the Qur'an:[16]

... that no bearer of burdens shall bear the burden of another. (53:38)

This verse must shock everyone who takes to heart the Christian principle of "loving thy neighbor," which seems to state the exact opposite.[17]

Yet verse 38 of surah 53 does not deal with a moral question at all. Rather, it makes two fundamental theological statements: it rejects the theory of original sin and the possibility of intercession. The latter completely delegitimizes the veneration of saints, denies the status of any type of clergy and the role of so-called sacraments, and rejects church hierarchies. A Muslim is the emancipated believer *par excellence*.

The refutation of the fatalism inherent in the idea of Original (or hereditary) Sin was of fundamental importance to me, because it also debunks the

---

16. See the story of my conversion to Islam, "Alhamdulillah, ein Muslim westlicher Herkunft," *Deutsche von Allah geleitet* (Cologne 1982).
17. The same statement is repeated in the following verses revealed later: 6:164; 17:15; 35:18; 39:7.

Christian teachings on salvation, incarnation, sacrificial death, and trinity. In time I began to realize how monstrous, even blasphemous it is to imagine that God could have fallen short in his creation; that He could have been unable to do anything about the disaster supposedly caused by Adam and Eve without begetting a son, only to have him sacrificed in such a bloody fashion; that God might suffer for mankind, His creation.

To me, it seemed as if Christianity was borrowing from atavistic myths, that both John the Evangelist and Dionysius Areopagita (whoever they were) laced it with neo-Platonic and Gnostic speculations thoroughly mixed by Philos in Alexandria, including mystical dreams of one Plotinus. With all that in mind, who can still call Mary "Mother of God"?

My eyes were opened to the unfortunate role Paul has been playing. He, who had never met Jesus, with his extreme christology replaced the original and correct Judeo-Christian view of Jesus as a Jewish reform Prophet in the tradition of Barnabas. I understood how the dogma pronouncing Jesus to be of the same as God, adopted in 325 by the 1st Ecumenical Council of Nicaea (under pagan chairmanship), had set Christianity off on a tragically wrong course. Only today, more than 1650 years after the fact, some courageous Christian theologians are in the process of setting the record straight, desperately trying to reinterpret the Nicene Creed or to bypass it altogether by returning to the sources. In short, I began to see Islam with its own eyes, as the unadulterated, pristine belief in the one and only, the true God, Who does not beget, and was not begotten, Whom nothing and nobody resembles (surah 112, *al Ikhlas*). I saw Islam as the undiluted original Abrahamic monotheism which had succeeded in avoiding both the Jewish and the Christian deviations: either to believe in an exclusive contractual agreement between God and His "chosen people," or to exalt a prophet through a subsequent process of deification.

In place of the qualified deism of a tribal God and the contradictory constructions of a divine Trinity, the Qur'an showed me the most lucid, most straightforward, the most abstract—thus historically most advanced—and least anthropomorphic concept of God. The Qur'an's ontological statements, as well as its ethical teachings, impressed me as profoundly plausible, "as good as gold," so there was no room for even the slightest doubt about the authenticity of Muhammad's prophetic mission. People who understand human nature cannot fail to appreciate the infinite wisdom of the "Dos and Don'ts" handed down from God to man in the form of the Qur'an.

Before my formal conversion, I had to deal with the widespread argument that changing one's religion was not worth the trouble, since all religions ended up worshipping the same God and preach the same morals anyway. Besides, was it not more important to do the right thing and to have God in one's own "private" heart, rather than praying five times a day, fasting, or going on a pilgrimage? How many times did I have to listen to these stereotypical apologetics from Turkish "Muslims" who could not face up to their loss of faith. Be that as it may, an irrelevant, private God is no God at all. And all of these arguments do not carry any weight if, and only if, we are convinced that God speaks to us in the Qur'an. Those who follow this conviction to its logical consequence have no other choice but to become Muslims—in the fullest sense of the word: somebody who surrenders himself to God, seeks refuge with Him and submits to His will as revealed in the Qur'an.

In this sense my eventual conversion (better perhaps: reversion) was inevitable—much like the practical consequences that were yet to follow.

FIVE TIMES A DAY
—AS DIRECTED

Before I pronounced my declaration of faith (*shahadah*) in 1980 (freshly bathed, as required) I may have been intellectually close to Islam, but I had not yet concerned myself much with the rules and regulatons which are to govern a Muslim's life. Intellectually I was a Muslim, yes, but not yet in practical terms. This now had to radically change. I had to become a Muslim, not just in my convictions, but also in my deeds.

If religion means man's link to God, and Islam submission to Him, then my most important obligation as a 50-year-old junior Muslim was to learn how to pray properly. One does not have to be a "computer freak" to understand that we are faced here with a communications problem: What kind of communication is *compatible* with Him?

There is certainly no other misbehavior which casts a greater doubt on somebody's commitment to Islam than interrupting contact with God. Because praising God inevitably becomes the central activity of someone who understands what it implies to say: "I believe in God." Ergo: Someone who does not pray I refuse to consider a Muslim.

A man who declares his love to a woman far away, but does not feel the need to call or write her and spends the entire day without looking at her picture—such a person is not really in love.

How this situation relates to prayer is obvious. An individual awakened to the full meaning of God's existence will feel the need to meditate frequently and address himself to God in all circumstances, practicing in fact what is called *taqwā*, God-awareness. This is the only way to fulfill what Muslims promise when reciting *Surat al Fatiḥah*:

You alone do we worship, and You alone do we ask for help. (1:5)

*

At the same time I was still ignorant of the prescribed elements of Islamic ritual prayer, not to mention the ability to recite in Arabic. Repairing these shortcomings was my top priority. Even before I started studying "The Prayer in Islam," arguably the most reliable and best illustrated German introduction,[18] I asked a Turkish friend of mine to show me how exactly to cleanse myself before prayer, how to stand, bow, and prostrate during ritual prayer, how to sit (on the left foot) and position one's arms, where to focus one's eyes, when to recite aloud and when silently (while still moving one's lips), how to position oneself behind the leader (imām), what to do when coming late, how to move among praying people in a mosque.

It is a veritable science! So much so that mere posing as a Muslim without having learnt to be one can be risky business!

*

Strange as it may sound, the Muslim prayer already begins in the bathroom or at the faucets in front of a mosque with the washing of hands, lower arms, face and neck, and with the rinsing of the mouth, blowing of one's nose and wetting of the hair.[19] This is a matter whose mastery in sequence and execution takes a whole lot of practice. How to wash one's hand, how to make sure that even the heels are washed—everything is laid down as meticulously as the liturgical gestures of a Catholic priest.

This is how the believer mentally prepares for prayer, mentally disengaging from everyday routine. The state of complete dedication to prayer is achieved when one begins prayer by raising one's hands up to either side of the head while exclaiming *"Allahu akbar"* (God alone is great). At least washing one's feet makes obvious hygienic sense, since people step barefoot on the rug on which they are about to prostrate. (Today, I find the thought rather unsavory that people may attend a Christian service unwashed.) On the other hand, applying cold water to one's lower arms has

18. Muhammad Ahmad Rassoul, *Das Gebet im Islam* (Cologne 1983).
19. This small ablution (*wudu*) is insufficient after sexual intercourse or menstruation. In these cases, the ritual purity is regained by washing the entire body (*ghusl*).

been stimulating blood circulation long before Father Kneipp propagated his "water cures."

In hot countries, ritual cleansing does not present a problem—one just dries quickly. In cold latitudes, however, when there's no towel around, slipping wet feet into socks can be quite uncomfortable. Whenever there is no water available, it is enough to perform a symbolic cleansing by patting the hands on dust and wiping the hands and face. This is called *tayamum.* I found myself in such a situation just once, when I was on a day trip to the oil rich Liwa region in the United Arab Emirates, on December 7, 1993. Our otherwise desert savvy driver got stuck in precisely the kind of sand that is suitable for an ersatz-cleansing.

*

Learning the formalities of ritual prayer was easier than expected, since it is composed of two regular building blocks called *rak'ah.* These fixed elements of prayer either conclude by standing up from the last prostration, or by sitting up. Immersed in prayer one can easily get confused, getting up while everybody else remains sitting. Fortunately, many imāms prevent such embarrassment by audibly stretching out their command (*"Allahu akbar"*) when sitting is in order.

In addition to that, one has to memorize the number of *rak'ah*s that constitute the morning, noon, afternoon, evening, and night prayers; and when they are to be performed. In addition, one has to learn which of these rules a traveler has to observe, and which not.

Finally I learnt that one assumes the proper prayer position by forming uninterrupted, straight files, one complete row after the other, women among women, men among men. The files are then closed by spreading the feet sideways so neighbors in a row touch each other. The symbolic force of this intended physical contact, not just incidental brushing, never ceases to impress me. Muslims at Prayer experience a much stronger sense of community than can possibly be alive in sparsely occupied church pews.

Upon conclusion of the prayer, this community manifests itself anew: Greeting one's neighbors "Peace be with you!" (*as salāmu 'alaykum,* in the plural), one turns first to the right, then to the left.

The former secretary general of Algerian foreign affairs once told me how as a child he once tried to improve this wishing of peace. It had seemed to him more logical to say: *"Assalāmu 'alaika"* (Peace be with you, in the singular). Whereupon he received a resounding box on the ear from his father. He learnt that Muslims always say "Peace be with you" in the plural, because it is meant to include every living thing, visible or invisible, angels as well as cockroaches.

It is very important to know how to "demarcate" the area one occupies for praying. For that purpose, people place their spectacles, wallets, or whatever is handy on the floor about 21/2 feet in front of them. Nobody will violate a zone so marked off, or walk in front of someone in prayer. On December 26, 1982, as I was about to leave the Prophet's Mosque in Madinah after the prayer, I ran into a crowd that was beginning to back up from the steps of the main portal. What was going on? A latecomer had decided to join the prayer in progress when reaching the portal, right on the steps. He took his time, making up whatever parts of the prayer he had missed. Therefore, in due respect, the stream of worshippers exiting the building parted around him like a river flowing around a boulder. Nobody would have dared to disturb the peace of his prayer by violating his rather awkward praying space. I saw something even more amazing in 1992 as I was circling the Ka'bah like thousands of other pilgrims. A tiny, delicate woman against better judgment decided to pray only a few yards away from the shrine; she was surrounded by four strong men who had linked arms to protect her. Again, the same nonreaction from the crowd. No complaints, no sneers, but respect.

Because of these rigid rules it can sometimes be difficult, even impossible to leave the mosque from one of the front rows before everybody else is leaving. Once in 1993, after the Friday prayer, I had to keep my hosts in Abu Dhabi waiting quite a long time because I could not find a legitimate way out of the mosque. To reach the exit, I would have had to pass in front of people who were still in prayer—and this is *makrūh* (disliked).

*

I like to pray by myself. This way, I can determine my own rhythm. Proceedings in the mosque are usually a bit speedy to accommodate the old most mosques an officially appointed imam is available for leading the prayer. When this is not the case, people gathering for prayer have to settle on someone to function as their *ad hoc* imām. As a rule, in a private house the host has this privilege. But one can delegate this honor to one of the guests. Whenever we came together in my residence in Rabat to break the fast, I routinely deferred to the Saudi ambassador, or to the chairman of the Istiqlal Party, Maître Muhammad Boucetta. On one curious occasion, however, I found myself in the role of imam.[20]

On October 10, 1985, while visiting San Francisco to attend the annual meeting of the North Atlantic Assembly, I searched phone books and church registries for a mosque. I was absolutely convinced that I would find an Islamic congregation in this American capital of sectarianism. I was, however, quite astonished to read: "Islamic Center, 850 Divisadero Street, daily service 12:00 P.M., Sundays 1 P.M.," as churches advertise which, unlike Muslims, do not schedule their services by the course of the sun. When I arrived, I found a black congregation consisting of just three members. In anticipation of the call to prayer, an old man with curly white hair was reading from an Arabic copy of the Qur'an, following each line with his finger, his glasses sliding down to the tip of his nose. Another member by the name of Yusuf Simon also showed up, a young black student of political science, and a Shi'ite. He responded with equanimity that by now he was used to discrimination: as a black man among whites, as a Muslim among Christians, and as a Shi'ite among Sunni Muslims.

I continued to be amazed when the *mu'adhdhin* commenced with the second call to prayer *(iqāmah)*, only to follow up with the longer, first call *(adhān)*. Considering that Bilal, Islam's very first *mu'adhdhin* in Madinah, had been a black man, I hesitated to correct his successor in San Francisco. And yet, I just could not let go by unchecked such heterodox developments, or could I? I gently began to explain that I had been to Makkah before, and that the call for prayers there were made in reverse order. Their reaction might have been surprising for non-Muslims, but appeared normal to me: at once the small congregation elected me to be their imām of the day, because they saw me as the more "knowledgeable" Muslim. The fact that I was German, white, and had only just dropped in off the street did not matter in the least. So I found myself in front of the prayer niche, silently won-

---

20. For more details, see Murad W. Hofmann, *Diary of a German Muslim* (Cologne 1987).

dering whether it at least had been correctly aligned toward Makkah, proceeded to straighten out the line of the mini-congregation behind me, and lifted my hands to begin with the prefatory *"Allahu akbar!"*

Knowledge alone is what counts. This accounts for another experience I had, in December, 1982, when a bright looking, barely 15-year-old Arab youngster led a group of obviously illiterate Pakistani pilgrims in prayer at the Madinah Sheraton.

Going to the mosque for the noontime prayer on Friday is a must. Essentially, it consists of two immediately consecutive sermons (*khutbah*) delivered by the same preacher (*khātib*). His speeches regularly lead up to an invocation and supplication to God. In the Muslim world it is still customary on this occasion to ask God's blessing and guidance for the current head of State, a practice which is of the highest political significance. Nonobservance may signal revolution.

For many years now, it has been my experience that these sermons in the Muslim world often fall short of their potential because they invariably tend to appeal to emotions at the expense of reason, preaching to the converted over and over again, rather than broadening the rational foundation of their faith. This shows in the modulation of the voice in particular. Much of the time, preachers shout at the top of their lungs as if to rally an army for the last decisive battle. On the other hand, I admit that sermons in the modern fashion of philosophical homilies would hardly be appropriate, because there is scarcely anybody in the Muslim world who would consider himself an atheist anyway. Why problematize the fundamentals of Islamic faith publicly if one can utilize pedagogically the remarkable acceptance of authority so typical of the Islamic world (and so incomprehensible in the West)? Even here we have notable exceptions. When I lived in Rabat, we used to do what I remembered many Christians doing in Munich: to go out of one's way in order to listen to a particular clergyman. On Friday we drove all the way to the city limits so we could hear the intellectually stimulating imām of the Lalla Sukaynah Mosque.

In the course of my career I was frequently privileged during Ramaḍan or the Festival of Sacrifice to pray behind heads of state like the Algerian president Shadli Benjedid and King Hassan II of Morocco. All of this in front of TV cameras and in compliance with protocol.

48

Hassan II welcomes Dr. Murad Hofmann to the celebration of 'Id al Fiṭr in the al Fahs Mosque

On all of these occasions I could sense how the Islamic prayer invests even such an illustrious ambiance with a democratic spirit. A king in stockings who prostrates himself on the floor is quite removed from a *Président de la France* who strides through Reims Cathedral to ascend his privileged perch.

*

The prayers—at least their obligatory text and the required Qur'an citations—have to be recited in Arabic. Some people have a harder time learning some of the smaller Qur'anic surahs or excerpts from larger ones than memorizing other formalities. For my part, I very much disliked memorizing transcribed Arabic texts, thus acting as a Catholic alterboy who does not know any Latin. Therefore, I decided to follow in the footsteps of virtually all other Muslims and learn at least as much Arabic as would be necessary to understand the grammatical forms and the etymology of the vocabulary. (When I became ambassador to Algeria, this elementary proficiency came in very handy.) Naturally, the first thing I learnt was the *Fatiḥah* ("The Opening"), the first surah of the Qur'an, which is an essential part of every prayer segment (*rak'ah*) and, therefore, had to be recited at least 17 times a day:

> In the name of Allah, the Most Gracious, the Most Merciful. Praise be to Allah, Master of the Universe; the Most Gracious, the Most Merciful, Lord of the Day of Judgment. You alone do we worship. And You alone do we ask for help. Guide us on the straight way, the way of those upon whom You have bestowed Your blessings, not of those who have been condemned, nor of those who go astray.

Then I learnt surah 112, *al Ikhlās,* which has only four short verses, but according to the Prophet contains a good third of the Qur'an's overall message.

> In the name of Allah, the Most Gracious, Most Merciful. Say: "He is Allah, the One and Only; Allah, the Eternal, Absolute; He begets not, nor is He begotten; and there is nothing comparable to Him.

The short surahs *al Falaq* (113) and *al Nās* (114), which begin by seeking protection, were next, followed by other brief Makkan surahs like *al Fil* (105), *Quraysh* (106), *al Kāfirūn* (109) and *al Nasr* (110), but I also learnt to recite the first Qur'anic revelation (verses 1–5 of the 96th surah, *al 'Alaq*):

> Read! In the name of your Lord Who created—created man out of something that clings. Read! For your Lord is the Most Generous, Who taught by means of the pen—taught man what he did not know.

But only after acquiring an advanced proficiency of Arabic did I dare approach longer passages, such as the Throne-Verse (2:255); the Light-Verse (24:35), as well as the section containing most of the "beautiful names" of God, i.e., the attributes of perfection (59:22–24).

A close scrutiny of the prayer texts reveals that praising God is at the heart of the ritual Islamic prayer—without excluding supplication. This corresponds to a statement in the Qur'an according to which mankind's ultimate purpose is to recognize God through its powers of perception and reflection, and to praise Him. This characterizes the Muslim's basic outlook. Just ask one how he is doing. He won't reply by saying "fine" or "it could be better," but simply answer "Praise be to God!" *(al ḥamdu lillah).*

After the ritual prayer, some like to pick up a string of either 33 or 99 prayer beads (*tasbiḥ*), or just use their fingers to continue praising God by repeating 33 times each of the following phrases: "All praise belongs to Allah" (*subḥan Allahu*), "Praise be to God" (*al ḥamdu lillah*), and "God alone is great" (*Allahu akbar*). Note: Contrary to the Christian litany, there is not even one single petition to God included in this habitual form of *dhikr* (repetitive remembrance of God).

But supplication does have its place. Not to petition God at all would be a form of blasphemy, since He assured us:

> I respond to the call of him who calls, whenever he calls Me. (2:186)

In particular, as instructed by the Qur'an the Muslim likes to pray:

> O Lord, give us good things in this world and good things in the other world, and save us from the fire of hell. (2:201)

These private prayers (*du'ā'*) are formless and not tied to time, place, or Arabic. Ideally, they grow into a continuous meditation about God (*dhikr* in the Sufi sense), a state of mind which Islamic mystics have forever been striving for. Annemarie Schimmel has collected a number of beautiful *du'ā's*.[21]

Islamic mysticism has helped to preserve the bond between outward form, social function, and the deep spirituality of Islamic prayer. Authentic Islamic mystics, from Ibn al 'Arabi, the 12th/13th century Andalusian Sufi, to the contemporary Frithjof Schuon,[22] have never dispensed with the formalities of the ritual, but spiritualized them considerably. Says Schuon, "The Muslim, especially the one following the Sunnah down its most remote pathways, lives in a weave of symbols."[23] Those who take this to heart will prevent their prayers from becoming a routine physical exercise.

Whether you are in the Shi'ite mosque located on Alster Lake in Hamburg, in a mosque made from trunks and leaves of palm trees in the

---

21.   Annemarie Schimmel, *Denn dein ist das Reich - Gebete aus dem Islam* (Freiburg 1978), and *Dein Wille geschehe - Die schönsten islamischen Gebete* (Bonndorf 1992).
22.   Frithjof Schuon, *Islam and the Perennial Philosophy* (London 1976).
23.   Frithjof Schuon, *Den Islam verstehen* (Understanding Islam) (Munich 1988), p. 85; about the spiritualization of Islam, see also Adel-Theodor Khoury, *Gebete des Islam* (Mainz 1981).

east Moroccan oasis of Figuig, or in the Umayad mosque in Damascus with its wealth of gold mosaics, the prayer is so uniform it is as if all Muslims had the same teacher. (They had.)[24] This uniformity provides a traveling Muslim with the peace and assurance indispensable for his focus and concentration during prayer, no matter where.

*

Apart from its spiritual side, Islamic prayer has quite a concrete, physical and potentially political component. It takes quite a while before one is able to relax on a hard floor sufficiently enough to avoid cramps; this is easier done barefoot than wearing socks, because these will twist and stretch. But to spend hours sitting quietly on the ground like our oriental brothers do, is an art that, in my more advanced years, I cannot hope to master anymore.

In addition to that, Islamic prayer is most certainly beneficial in taking on the modern day symptoms of stress, whose causes are easily identified: People today do not work physically as hard and as much as they used to—rather the opposite is true. New is the acceleration of all operational procedures—by fax, e-mail, internet, cellular phone, and express-couriers—which causes subordinates (bosses to a lesser degree) to feel overwhelmed, to develop the sinking feeling of losing control, of being cornered by deadlines, of *failure*, pure and simple. Alcohol, nicotine, sleeping pills and stimulants worsen the condition. The costs (of heart attacks) among high-level managers are running so high that top people are ordered to go on vacation, that leadership seminars talk about bio-feedback and Transcendental Meditation (T.M.), and people discover Japanese tea ceremonies for themselves.

It is my contention that Islamic prayer does all of this—and much more. Not only does it help the faithful to unwind, but also to gain the necessary inner independence from a preoccupation with money, fame, and career. While stressed-out Americans see themselves confronted by the alternative of "fight" or "flight," Muslims avail themselves of a third option: "going

---

24.   Shi'ite Muslims and Sunni Muslims of the North African Malikite rite do not fold their arms across their chest during prayer but let their arms hang naturally—a minor variation within unity.

with the flow." Thanks to the Islamic tradition of prayer, no true Muslim can be stressed, and a person under stress cannot be a genuine Muslim.

I know what I'm talking about. From 1979 to 1983 I ran the bureau of NATO and Defense Affairs of the German Foreign Office; and from 1983 to 1987, I was a particularly high assassination risk as Director of Information for the North Atlantic Alliance in Brussels—all of which subjected me to all possible stress-inducing factors.

Beginning in 1980, however, I never went on my official trips without a prayer rug and a compass (made in Taiwan) to determine the direction of prayer, knowing full well that a clean towel is all it really takes, and that "to God belong the east and the west, so wherever you turn yourselves, there is Allah's countenance (2:115)." Increasingly, my days were structured around prayer times and not driven by a clock that is generating a hectic rush. (For that reason, appointments with Muslims are not made for "three fifteen" sharp, but for the slightly more indefinite time "after the midday prayer," or "after the evening prayer."

In other words, prayer showed me the way to the kind of equanimity and inner independence that seems to shield Muslims from the constraints and duress of the material world (*al dunya*), because they can stop the world after all and get off—by escaping from an environment where time is money, and money is everything.

In 1992, at the time when the German media's anti-Islamic defamation campaign against me was at a fever pitch, many of my colleagues could not understand (or interpreted it as arrogance) that I would take so little notice of that. The explanation could have been found in the 5th verse of the above quoted *Sūrat al Fatiḥah.*

By now, the prayer's structuring quality has become so important to me that I would not want to live in a country where I could not hear the *mu'adhdhin*'s call to prayer as beautifully as in Fez or as loud as, until recently, in Istanbul.

*

I frequently had a chance to observe how the essentially harmless act of praying can grow into a political controversy. In 1988, even before the Front for Islamic Salvation (F.I.S.) in Algeria entered the public arena, its followers had begun to avoid mosques run by the government. (In much the same way as Turkish guest workers in Germany tend to stay away from institutions sponsored by the Turkish Office of Religion.) Their "parallel Islam" manifested itself also in parallel prayer. For example, in 1987, while visiting friends in Blida, we prayed among ourselves in a private residence next door to a big mosque.

It was also highly significant to see how groups of young people in Algiers would enter the mosque not much before or after the midday prayer so that they could pray seperately, in a corner, and not behind the State-appointed imām. In September 1994, I observed the same symptom in the Sinan Pascha Mosque of Beşiktaş, a popular and proudly Muslim neighborhood in Istanbul.

Also, in October 1997, I observed in a mosque of Baḥrain that Shi'ite Muslims would conduct their separate prayer, in parallel to the one lead by a Sunni imām. For political cohesion, these are alarming symptoms. On the Festival of Sacrifice in 1988, the Algerian government decided to prove in the Fisherman's Mosque near the port of Algiers how truly religious it and the F.L.N. Party were becoming. But people became outraged (or amused) when on TV they witnessed that top officials of the State and Party did not even know how to pray properly. They had not taken off their glasses, and thus were unable to touch the ground with forehead and nose simultaneously. A few months later, in October, the F.L.N. was ousted by a popular rebellion, and the F.I.S. was recognized as a legal party. Speaking about the political potential of prayer.

A lot remains to be said about this, but at this very moment, sounding from dozens of loudspeakers in Beşiktaş, Teşvikiye, Nişantaş, Yildīz, and Levent, is the call to evening prayer, and this has to be performed immediately after sunset, without delay.

SOBERINGLY SOBER

In public my becoming a Muslim had become most evident in my polite refusal of alcohol, as well as in the disappearance of the customary bottle of red wine from my dinner table. In the beginning, I felt that I would not sleep well without a swig of alcohol in my system, or that without it, I would have a difficult time falling asleep. On the contrary! Since my body did not have to break down alcohol, I slept far better than ever before, with a lower heart rate. Naturally, alcohol as a digestive for fatty foods would have been very nice and beneficial indeed, but we had banned pork from our table anyway, and I had been developing a sickening revulsion against the mere smell of this highly unwholesome and downright unhealthy meat.

*

During my personal days of *jāhiliyah*, my own pre-Islamic "time of dark ignorance," I had made a cult of the wonderful, unique red Burgundy wines to such an extent that I was able to identify many of the Côte d'Or's *grands crus* by my palate alone. "Masculine" wines like a Chambertin or Grands Echézeaux can be easily distinguished from "feminine" ones, such as Vosne-Romanée or Musigny. But being able to distinguish further among those *appelations* requires a sense of taste discriminating enough to identify the etheric oils as well as the minerals which are characteristic of each famous vineyard. The resulting bouquet or aroma can be suggestive of chestnuts, truffles, vanilla, raspberry or bramble, but also of earth, metal or moor. My diplomatic life gave me ample opportunity to hone these skills, primarily during gala diners at the conclusion of NATO conferences at ministerial level.

I "practiced" diligently my admired ability to discern a Clos de Bèze from a Bonnes Mares grown nearby; for that purpose I even spent "wine vacations" between Dijon and Beaune. In 1967, while posted in Paris, I would frequently consult a Guide Michelin to reserve a table at a one-star restaurant. While doing so, I would select the wine over the phone and ask for the bottle to be opened right away to allow the wine to sufficiently oxidize in order to reach its full maturity by the time I walked through the restaurant door. There I would choose my menu to go with the wine, not the other way around.

In 1977/78, as a widowed Minister Counceler 1st class and DCM (Deputy Chief of Mission) at the (West) German embassy in Belgrade, I hosted wine tasting sessions, offering German white wine from the Nahe river region. I presented almost colorless but rarely dry wines from the Winery of Viktor Golling, grown in Bad Münster, Bad Kreuznach and Bretzenheim. The idea (and pleasure) was to demonstrate to my guests that different grapes (e.g. Riesling, Scheurebe, Traminer), soil (e.g., slate), harvesting times (Auslese, Spätlese, Beerenauslese, "ice wine"), methods of fermentation (stopping it with or without sulfur), and climatic changes from year to year can be identified with one's palate. Devoted teacher that I am, I offered a succession of six or seven wines where each one had something in common with the previous sample, yet was sufficiently distinct in other ways. And indeed: some of my guests developed the ability to distinguish between spicy, fruity, heavy, steely, earthy, flat or rich wines, and also to match these traits with the elements discussed before.

*

But when the time came, I considered the Qur'anic prohibition of alcohol and other drugs[25] not just a social necessity, but also a source of moral enrichment and improvement. Indeed, it is a matter of human dignity to be at all times of a sound mind, and in permanent sobriety—soberness as a state of mind. Overnight, once and for all, I put an end to my questionable expert career as Chevalier de Tastevin. Man prides himself, claiming to be the crown of creation, for possessing self-awareness and the ability to think rationally. We can reflect and act reasonably. It is precisely these ennobling qualities which we are systematically destroyed with our structural alcoholism and drug addiction. We are degrading ourselves within the cosmic

---

25. About the Qur'anic history of the prohibition of addictive substances in several consecutive stages see Helmut Gätje, *Koran und Koranexegese* (Stuttgart 1971), pp. 264–276.

hierarchy and fall below the always sober animal world. To be cruelly frank: Alcoholism and drug addiction amount to intellectual self-mutilation. My Serbian housekeeper, an inveterate alcoholic, kept relapsing over and over again—passing out in the kitchen and smashing her glasses as the guests were arriving—and thus set a cautionary example for me.

In any case, alcoholics are a truly miserable, undignified, and depressing sight. They are committing suicide by degrees, fully aware of it, but unable to fight their way out, because alcohol robs them of their last bit of resolve.

In the modernist middle and upper class society of the major Turkish cities—Istanbul, Izmir, Ankara—one finds even more alcoholics than in Germany. As early as noon, they are clinging to their Raki-glasses, the other hand holding the indispensable cigarette, proving perhaps that they are good "emancipated" Kemalsits, but also proving that they are not their own masters anymore. They are, in a theological sense, indulging in some kind of *shirk* because alcohol and nicotine are more important to them than anything else in the world—God included. They can do without Him, but not without Raki. Or so they believe.

With its unconditional prohibition of addictive substances, the Qur'an seeks to fight even the supposedly harmless, seemingly controllable beginnings of a gradually developing addiction: the one "harmless glass" which one day is bound to become the one glass too many. It is typical for addicts to consider themselves in *contro,* pretending they can stop any time if they wished. But that is mere self-delusion. They have an inexhaustible inventory of excuses as to why they have to smoke or drink at this very moment: because they are happy, or sad; under stress, or on vacation; at a party or lonely; sick, or feeling good; hungry or very full.

As "boss" of the embassy responsible for the supervision of my coworkers, drawing a line, presented an acute problem, even an insoluble dilemma for me: If I warned a colleague only one day too early of his or her alcohol abuse, I would violate his individual right to self-determination (and consequently, get into legal trouble with the labor union). But as early as the next day, the same union officials might readily admit that the colleague in question had, indeed, become a professional drinker. In a soundbite second, he or she became officially recognized as an alcohol victim, an now again under legal protection, this time for being "sick."

Sober people who find themselves among merrymakers can sometimes feel completely out of place, even at the most convivial party, especially since people who drink think of themselves as particularly witty, able, and full of imagination. As a jazz percussionist, I had ample opportunity to prove the contrary to myself—by using myself as a Guinea pig, as it were. On my Premier drum set I accompanied the same musical pieces three times in a row: "The Hucklebuck" by Buck Clayton, the "Royal Garden Blues" (Bix Beiderbecke version), and finally—but only with brushes—the Ella Fitzgerald and Louis Armstrong duet, "Can't We Be Friends," and recorded myself every time. But in between each session I had a double Bourbon of my favorite brand, that smoky Jack Daniels. I was convinced that my jazz drumming was becoming more ingenious every time. But alas, when I was sober again the honest tape revealed to my ears the crushing truth.

I was especially mortified over the behavior of some of my compatriots on a Lufthansa flight to Jeddah. The closer the frightfully dry Saudi Arabia came, the faster they called the steward for more whiskey—up to four of those little bottles at a time—as if one could stockpile intoxication. It was really shameful to see them staggering out of the airplane in Jeddah, shrink-wrapped Christmas tree in hand.

Experiences like that convinced me that there does not seem to be a larger obstacle to the spread of Islam in Germany than the Qur'an's prohibition of pork and alcohol. This is the real problem, and not people's shrinking belief in divine incarnation or trinity. Currently there is no way that the average Bavarian will renounce his pork knuckles and strong brew, and the natives of Cologne certainly will not be robbed of their Kölsch beer with a shot of Schnaps.

As early as the 18th century, German writer Gotthold Ephraim Lessing made the following telling point:

> The Turks have beautiful daughters - its true!
> And keen-eyed guardians of virtue;
> Whoever wants, can marry one, two, three:
> A Turk! That's what I'd like to be!
> How would I want for love to strive
> And lead, in love, a peaceful life.
> But wait! - they don't drink any wine;
> To be a Turk? That won't be fine.

By the way, becoming a Turk still would not be worth Lessing's while. They do drink wine today, but marrying several beautiful daughters is against the law in today's Turkey.

During social gatherings, Muslims—nonsmokers most of the time and clutching a glass of water or juice—often come across as spoilsports, or worse, as one obtrusive personified moral reproach. Lessing also captured this sentiment in a poignant little verse, the point of which I obviously don't share:

> It seems that here, Paul, you're the only drunk I see,
> By wanting to be sober, which no one wants to be.

Which is why my wife and I are receiving fewer and fewer invitations to private festivities and dances—as if it were impossible to have a good time without alcohol. (Muslim weddings prove the opposite.) We are being *made* outsiders. Then again, does the Qur'an not recommend to keep the company of like-minded people, of Muslims, anyway?

A frequently heard rebuttal of both the Islamic prohibition of intoxicating substances and pork, is the argument that those proscriptions had been climate related and, therefore, make no sense in our climatized, air-conditioned, and refrigerated era. This absurd argument flies in the face of the fact that the incidence of alcohol-related damage in our technological era eclipses the 7th century by far! Back then, a drunk could fall off his horse, beat wife and child, and sever a camel's tendons. (It was precisely such a nasty incident that found its way into one of the three Qur'anic passages dealing with alcohol.)[26]

Today, alcoholic stupor is still leading to chronic abuse of women and children. But these days airplanes can fall from the sky because of inebriation, and the intoxicated skipper of an Exxon tanker has caused the largest environmental catastrophe to date. The human and financial damage inflicted by structural addiction in the western world cannot possibly be tabulated, notwithstanding all available statistics on traffic and workplace accidents. At some Turkish clinics the units for the treatment of alcoholics are located next to the psychiatric wards, serving as a warning of the usual progress that takes alcoholics over to the station next door.

---

26.   2:219; 4:43; 5:90 f.—revealed in this order.

I am myself a victim of drunken driving. After an academic year at Union College in Schenectady, New York, I traveled through the United States as a hitchhiker. On June 28, 1951, we had a very bad accident near Holy Springs (Mississippi). Traveling on the Interstate from Atlanta (Georgia), we had been closing in on our next stop, Memphis on the Mississippi, when all of a sudden a shadow was directly upon us. That is all I remember.

Later on, I learnt that we had a head-on collision with a vehicle which like a "ghost driver" was traveling on our side of the highway. The driver and his passenger had been to Tennessee, a state which allows the sale of alcohol, in order to "fill'er up" before returning back to the "dry" state of Mississippi.

At the hospital, it turned out that we had actually been dealt the better deck, since our sturdier, pre-war 1941 Chevrolet had run into a Chevy built in the war year of 1943. Evidently the dislocation of my arm, which I had slung over the backrest, had served like a safety belt. But it was also quite evident that I would not have survived had I been shorter by only three inches. In that case, going at the combined speed of about 100 mph I would not have smashed my mouth and teeth, but the nose and eye section of my face with deadly consequence. As it is, I got away leaving nineteen teeth behind.

After sewing up my chin and my lower lip, the surgeon comforted me somewhat clumsily by saying that I could patch up my disfigured face in a couple of years with cosmetic surgery. He offered a further consolation: "Under normal circumstances, no one survives an accident like that. God has something special in mind for you, my friend!" I was thinking about what that could be as I was limping through Holy Springs, looking for a way to give myself a treat on my 20th birthday, with my arm in a sling, a bandaged knee, an iodine-discolored, stitched-up lower face, and—thank God—morphine in my blood. Eating, drinking, strolling, scaring off gawking kids, answering questions—everything was equally painful. I ended up indulging in a haircut—at least that did not hurt.

Finally, thirty years later, on the very day I professed my faith in Islam, the true meaning of my survival became clear to me.

ON THE PROVING GROUND

A few months after embracing Islam, it was with some trepidation that I was looking forward to Ramaḍan—the month of fasting and the ninth month of the Islamic lunar calendar. It is an endurance test where every Muslim pushes his everyday sobriety to the hilt. For 29 or 30 days, from dusk to dawn, I was supposed to abstain from eating, drinking, smoking, and sexual activity, while at the same time doing my days work as usual.[27]

My first encounter with the true meaning of fasting happened in 1977 on a Yugoslav JAT fight from Belgrade to Istanbul. After my neighbor in the economy class had his dinner tray served, he just sat there, without touching his food. Occasionally glancing at his watch he waited until shortly after tables were being cleared and the time for breaking the fast (*iftar*) had arrived.

In Belgrade, we frequently invited our gardener, Ramadani Ramadan, for an *iftar* meal, because we felt sorry for his steadfast, obstinate insistence on fasting. Come daybreak, once he was able to tell a white piece of yarn from a black one, he refused to have one morsel of food. Compassion once moved me to join in on his fasting, at least for a week. But alas, rehearsing Ramaḍan is an exercise in futility; a 30-day fast can only be mastered by fasting for 30 days.

My duties in the Foreign Office in Bonn occasionally included organizing working lunches for foreign guests given by the chief of my subdivision. I felt always slightly awkward when during Ramaḍan—while seated at the table—I could not join the meal. Did I have an upset stomach? Was the meal I had ordered not good enough for me? On that score, it was much easier to turn down juice or Turkish coffee whenever I made a demarche in the Yugoslav Foreign Office during Ramaḍan. Even the most hardened communist from Bosnia, Hercegovine, Macedonia, the

---

27. For more details, see: Affif A. Tabbarah, *The Spirit of Islam, Doctrine and Teachings* (Beirut 1988), pp. 154–159.

Sanjak of Novi Pazar or Kosova had sentimental memories of the Ramaḍans of his youth.
It is true that fasting during Ramaḍan becomes an exciting and eagerly awaited experience only in a Muslim environment: a month suffused with religion, introspection, and brotherhood.

*

Just like any other religious ritual, fasting in Islam (ṣawm) has two inseparable components: a spiritual and a physical one. The physical sacrifice begins in the morning, when it becomes harder to rise and shine without one's usual coffee or tea. In the course of the day, the blood sugar tends to take a noticeable dip so that one risks slacking off altogether. On the other hand, it is during Ramaḍan when people gain a particularly good sense of their biological clock. I, for instance, invariably experience a high at both 11 A.M. and 4 P.M., whether I am fasting or not. I made systematic use of this fact by prioritizing my deskwork according to which matters *must, should, or can* be attended to. Wherever possible, I processed the first batch of files when, as if somehow programmed, my biological high signaled normal blood pressure. Especially, way back when I was driving a Porsche 924 during Ramaḍan, it was of critical importance that I reminded myself over and over again to maintain a safe distance to less powerful cars on my eight mile ride each way between our home in Ixelles and NATO-Headquarters in Evère, a trip which also took me right through Brussels. With reflexes slowed down by fasting, I did not want to endanger myself or anybody else. As a matter of fact, traffic accidents rise sharply during Ramaḍan, above all because of so many fathers and sons speeding home from work simultaneously lest the family's festive breaking of the fast be delayed.

In 1993, five of my compatriots from the new German federal states (*Länder*) perished near Kéntira, north of Rabat. On February 25, the critical third day of the fast, a Moroccan bus driver had botched a passing attempt and ran into their bus, slicing up its side and causing it to flip over. His risky maneuver obviously was due to a lack of concentration brought about by fasting. (On the next day, when my wife and I visited the survivors, dispersed to several hospitals, we did not even try to explain to them that they had become victims of a *religious* practice.)

The third day of fasting is critical because it is the day when one is likely to feel worst, when low blood pressure causes splitting headaches, and the stomach might be upset—a situation which becomes even more severe when lying down. From this point on, however, our amazingly adaptable body begins to adjust to the new situation. Hunger and headaches disappear, and it is possible to watch other people eat without the least bit of food envy. However, after 16 or 17 hours without food, one may become so apathetic that one is incapable of reading the Qur'an and spends the last hour before *iftar* as a couch potato in front of the TV. In due course, an aversion to meat is also beginning to develop.

*

Nevertheless, each evening it is a real event when the end of the hours of fasting is marked by a cannon salute, as is the custom in the Islamic world. At that point before the evening prayer, we treat our body with a sip of water, juice, or almond milk and with an (odd) number of dates or olives, thanking Allah for giving us the strength to endure the rigors of fasting.

In Algeria and Morocco, *iftar* meals every single day begin with green peppermint tea (*shay bin-na'na'*) and the same, very nourishing dark soup, in Algeria called *shorba friq*, in Morocco known as *harira*, tasting slightly different in each individual family. In addition to that, people have a boiled egg, more dates, as well as candy laced with honey, the Prophet's own favorite. Before you know it, your body feels fully reinvigorated, like a watered flower.

After a brief pause, what follows is a complete meal with meat—in the Maghrib, with dishes like olive-chicken, roasted lamb, couscous with beef, tarts, and fruit. But these rich meals are over so fast that whenever I was invited for *iftar* at 7:30 P.M., I found myself back home no later than 9 P.M.

My understanding of Ramadan is based on the Sunnah and, unfortunately, does not agree with the customary practices in some Muslim countries, the Maghrib among them. People there have a tendency to make up at night what they were missing during the day. They watch vulgar TV shows and play cards late into the night—sometimes (God forbid!) even with alco-

63

hol—and at midnight a sumptuous third meal is served. As a consequence, many Algerians and Moroccans sleep too little, and on a full stomach—not too good either—so that they oversleep the morning prayer—during Ramaḍan of all times. The next morning, they are hardly able to function and doze off during working hours. This, in turn, fosters this curious tendency to simply exchange night and day. Thus Ramaḍan can degenerate into an additional consumerist month of vacation—a travesty.

In such countries, the sales of groceries actually go up during Ramaḍan. One thing, however, goes down for sure: job performance. Against such abuses it is to nobody's surprise when secular minded Arab leaders complain openly that their developing countries cannot "afford" the absenteeism and low working morale of Ramaḍan anymore.

I found it particularly absurd whenever people of very high social rank invited me to an *iftar* meal furnished with golden utensils (even though Islam already frowns upon tableware made of silver!). In such homes, after exchanging a hearty "enjoy your meal!" they would say, "In the name of the God!" (*bismillah*)—whereupon guests and hosts alike would dig into their luxury seafood without first performing the required evening prayer. It always seemed incongruous to me that people who do not pray still went to the trouble of fasting. Yet this behavior illustrates very well the fact that in parts of the Muslim world Ramaḍan has become quite detached from its *religious*, Islamic background, only to emerge as a constituent element of Muslim "civilization." This may account for the rather bizarre behavior of many a Muslim who abstains from alcohol only during Ramaḍan—one month of Islam, followed by eleven months of recuperation from it.

*

From 1987 to 1994, my own daily schedule during Ramaḍan was quite different. I would go to bed after evening prayers, at about 11 P.M. My alarm set for—let us say—3:30 A.M., i.e., 40 minutes before the renewal of fasting. This allowed me—as recommended by the Prophet—to eat a small meal (*suhur*) consisting of muesli, a banana, and lots of water before the morning cannon was fired. The remaining time before dawn I spent in the traditional way by reading the Qur'an. After the morning prayer, during which I renewed my intention to fast and asked for strength for it, I would rest for another couple of hours. Since the Muslims in my embassy would continue to work through lunch, they started working an hour later. As a matter of fact, I was able to move more files into my out-box than during normal times, if only because work helps to take one's mind off one's empty stomach. Also during Ramaḍan, I attended the monthly working luncheons with my colleagues from member countries of the European Union with an empty plate in front of me. In a politically adroit gesture my French colleague in Rabat, M. de Coignac, followed suit in order to "show his solidarity with the people of his host country," as he put it.

As a rule, in Rabat I concluded my working day during Ramaḍan by attending a religious lecture in the Royal Palace (*al durūs al Hasaniyah*). The entire Moroccan government, the general staff, prominent Muslim scholars ('ulama), as well as the accredited Muslim ambassadors congregated in the palace each day at around 5 P.M. While waiting for the king and the princes to arrive, we would be listening to the most accomplished Qur'an recitations, presented mainly by specialists from Indonesia. The lecturer of the day and his colleagues, who had been invited from every corner of the Islamic world, including American Muslims like Khalid Yaḥya Blankenship and illustrious authorities like the Egyptian Grand Mufti Shaykh Tantawi—now Shaykh al-Azhar—were seated on and around a traditional teacher's chair. The king sat with us in a square at the lecturer's feet.

My Muslim colleagues and I took turns organizing the subsequent *iftar* meal for around 7 P.M. Whenever, it was "my turn," the foyer of my residence in Souissi was decked out with clean carpets and prayer rugs. Thus the space between the banquet room and the *salon* area became transformed into a small mosque (*masjid*) or prayer room (*muṣallā*). The personal ties I was able to establish and cultivate on these occasions with cabinet ministers and royal advisors were very special and long lasting.

Over the duration of the fast I usually lost ten to fourteen pounds, settling into my ideal weight.

*

There is a spiritual component to the physical act of fasting without which it would become a mere feat of temporary starvation.

The month of fasting possesses a special dignity due to its historical significance. It was in Ramaḍan when the battle of Badr was fought (622), a crucial event for the survival of the initial Islamic community. But even more significant was the fact that it was in Ramaḍan, during the fateful "Night of Power (or Destiny)" (*laylat al qadr*), that the Qur'anic revelation began. This is what Surah 97 says about this event, usually commemorated during the 27th night of Ramaḍan:[28]

> In the name of Allah, the Most Gracious, the Most Merciful.
> We have indeed sent it down in the Night of Power.
> And what will let you know what is the Night of Power?
> The Night of Power is better than a thousand months.
> Therein come down the angels and the Spirit by
> permission of their Lord for every task:
> Peace she[29] is until the rise of dawn.

Certainly a text for meditation.

The *Lailat al Qadr*—with faint echoes of "Christmas," since gifts are exchanged *(zakat al fitr)*—is traditionally celebrated with long prayers *(tarāwih)*, recitations, speeches, and spiritual songs. If not on a night like this, when else would the true meaning of prophecy and divine revelation open eyes and minds?

*

Fasting in the month of Ramaḍan is every Muslim's duty. They consider it an obligation owed to God (*'ibadah*), one of the five "pillars" of Islam, which do not need any utilitarian justification. As a servant of his Lord the Muslim is fasting simply because He wants it so. It is a matter of obedience, and that settles it.

At the same time, it does not take a lot to realize that this rule as well, like all norms, is not made *for* God, but *by* God, for the benefit of mankind.

Ever since being thin is back in fashion, women in particular have been going through beauty diets that come close to extended Ramaḍan fasting and can even lead to anorexia. After all, word has gotten around about the

---

28. The new day in Islam begins at dusk.
29. In Arabic, the night is of feminine gender.

risks of cholesterol and overweight, hence the marketing of regimens for dieting and purification.

Fasting in Islam provides these benefits, and then some. For instance, it stirs the social conscience for those among us who have to "fast" the entire year due to a lack of food or money. At least once a year we are made to walk in their shoes.

For me, the most important side effect of Ramadan is having the opportunity to find out whether I am master of myself, or if I have become a slave to trifle habits. Without self-control, I would indeed cease to be a Muslim. I hope it is not from vanity, but out of sheer relief when on the last day of Ramadan, during the evening prayer, I rejoice, "I made it, with God's help!"

But who can tell me when exactly Ramadan begins and ends? Nowadays there should not be any difficulty at all for astronomy to calculate in advance when and where the new moon will appear. This is indeed the case—and yet, to their disgrace, Muslims in different continents often begin and end their fasting on different days, depending on whether they are Turks, Moroccans, or Saudis. This deprives the Muslim community from experiencing their universality and frequently opens Muslims to ridicule.

There are two reasons for this. For one, the Ummah is split by nationalist sentiments to a degree that it is not enough for Turks or Moroccans to know that the new moon has been sighted in Makkah. No way, it has to happen in Konya or Fez! This can easily shift the beginning and/or end of Ramadan by one day, since the sun-moon configuration is indeed different on every point of the globe. Unlike sunrise, which varies only by one or two minutes per day, the moonrise can vary by as much as 15 minutes from day to day.[30]

The second reason is best understood by lawyers. In early Islam, the coming event of the new moon was not determined by calculation or prognostication, but rather recognized with the naked eye. Then as today, to do so has never been a problem thanks to the extremely dry climate on the Arab peninsula, resulting in beautifully clear skies. Based on this orthodox procedure, Islamic legal scholars have concluded that determining the new

---

30. See G.S.P. Freeman-Grenville, *The Islamic and Christian Calenders*, 2nd edition, (Reading 1995).

moon, signaling the beginning of Ramaḍan, is not a matter of fact alone, but requires conformity to a procedure as well: that two reliable and independent witnesses confirm to have seen the new moon with their own eyes. This rejection of astronomical data corresponds to criminal procedure according to which a court must not admit evidence obtained by improper means.[31]

Orthodox believers are intent on abiding by the traditional procedure even in cases where the new moon phase has undoubtedly arrived, but cannot yet be sighted everywhere due to cloudy skies. The possible consequence of this approach became evident in 1994, when fasting in Morocco lasted *two* days longer than in Saudi Arabia. When tv pictures of the *'Id al fiṭr* celebrations in Makkah reached satellite dishes in Morocco, where people were continuing their fast for a 31st day, many of the proverbial "simple people" called this show of disunity scandalous. Is it really not possible, they argued, for everybody to follow the astronomical charts established for Makkah, which is already the accepted, natural practice for setting the dates of the *hajj* pilgrimage, and therefore, also for the Festival of Sacrifice (*'Id al aḍha*)?

When the end of Ramaḍan is celebrated (*'Id al-fiṭr*), the first breakfast cup of coffee in 29 or 30 days is a veritable, a major treat. During the ʿid-prayer, early in the morning, there is an aura of inner bliss about each and every person at the mosque.

It sounds absurd, but it is true: Having breakfast in the morning makes hungry at noon! During Ramaḍan, however, even without breakfast one forgets all about lunch.

And so everything goes back to normal.

Yet one thing remains available all year round: my "Ramaḍan button." During the year, whenever it becomes necessary to skip a meal or two, I push a mental button which psychologically transports me right back to Ramaḍan, instantly conjuring up its prevailing feelings and habits. Just like that! Immediately being hungry will seem negligible, and quite normal.

It may sound unbelievable but I am looking forward to the next Ramaḍan.

---

31.   See Abdelhamid Bentchikou, *The Time of Islam* (English, French, Arabic), loc. cit. 1991.

AT A TABLE WITH MUSLIMS

Since the last chapter discussed *not* eating, it is about time to point out that Muslims are not just eating, but meant to enjoy food, everything that is healthful. This covers everything, except pork (including the meat from the wild boar) and "dead meat" (carrion). Food products made from animal blood, such as blood sausages, or from pork, such as gummy bears, are definitely out, as are liquor-filled chocolates.

It is a mistake to assume that the Qur'an prohibits pork only for climatic reasons or because of the inability to deal with trichinosis in the 7th century. Today we know that pork is a contributing cause of colon cancer, arthritis, eczema and boils, as well as clogging of the arteries. Due to an abundance of histamines it can trigger nettle-rash fever; and it should give us pause to know that through the summer months the pig harbors the influenza virus.[32]

The title of this chapter, "At a Table with Muslims," is actually somewhat misleading. The fact is that not only desert nomads but also many of my fellow German Muslims eat on the floor or ground and not at a table. For instance, whenever we eat at the House of Islam in the Odenwald Forest village of Lützelbach, Germany, we roll out a mat in the conference hall or prayer room. We are then half sitting half *lying* through the meal, quite like the ancient Greeks, but without their wine. One eats in a reclining position by stretching one's legs out to the right, while the weight is supported with the left arm. This way, the right hand can be used to eat with. For right handed people, this is the only hand that can be used.[33] Many Western Muslims do this in order to emulate even unessential habits of the very man to whom they owe so much: Muhammad. There comes symbolism with

---

32. See Hans-Heinrich Reckeweg, *Schweinefleisch und Gesundheit* (Baden-Baden 1977).
33. A left-handed person can of course eat with his left, as long as unsanitary activites are performed exclusively with his or her right hand.

this mat: it reminds us that in this world we are all nomads, always on our journey back to God.

This is a very handy affair indeed, because rolling up and carrying off a mat is easier than making a table dissapear or stowing it away in a car. Therefore, the space where the mat is placed for meals remains a convenient multipurpose area. However: eating in a crouched, kneeling or reclining position tends to constrict the stomach, which is rather less convenient.

Occasionally even Arabs eat standing up, much like Westerners at a hot dog stand. In Algeria for one, it is the custom to eat roasted lamb (*mashwi*) while standing around the table. (In their efforts to pry off pieces of meat beginners can really get their fingers burnt.) The sides merely consist of flat rounds of bread, onions, salt and cumin. In all other Arab countries, however, people prefer to eat their lamb comfortably sitting down.

To eat standing up may well conform to the Sunnah, but *drinking* while standing definitely does not, since the Prophet expressly advised against this. This was of course way before the time when the cocktail party—the standing party *par excellence*—became fashionable also in Arabia.

*

From the Islamic point of view, a reasonable diet to keep body and soul together is as much a duty to oneself as it is to one's family; and therefore, it is also an act of serving God—worship in the sense of obedience. This is why Muslims begin their meals by pronouncing the *basmalah*, the formula "In the name of God!" *(bismillah)*, and conclude it by praising God with the phrase *al ḥamdu lillah*. Since the consumption of a meal is considered worship, it is not interrupted even when the *mu'adhdhin* calls everyone to a different kind of service, the prayer, as long as there will be enough time left for it after the meal.

And precisely because eating is a kind of worship, one takes care not to eat too much. Tradition teaches to stop eating before one feels full; it eschews satisfaction as a matter of principle. Rarely will a Muslim be caught stuffing his mouth.

At any rate, people are always ready to welcome unexpected guests. Islamic tradition states that in such cases food for two will suffice for three, and a meal for three will feed five. Because this is so, visitors in Muslim countries do not feel any compunction calling on families during meal times, thereby trying what Americans know as their "pot luck."

Having hosted many official functions in the Arab world, my wife and I learnt a thing or two about that. In this cultural region you never know who will show up at the dinner table on any given evening. Guests who had agreed and confirmed to come may let you down. This is unpleasant enough, but should more guests show up than invited for a seated dinner, the host may be put into an extremely awkward spot. If the number of guests exceeds the capacity of the dinner table, card tables will have to be brought in, a situation which is embarrassing for hosts and guests alike.

Structural uncertainties such as these have contributed to the image of the "unreliable Arab," and forced us to avoid formal "seated" dinners wherever possible, replacing them by more flexible "buffet" dinners. This way one can easily adjust to a shifting number of guests

There can be many reasons why an Arab guest fails to show up for dinner despite prior confirmation. Apart from work-related reasons, he could have been surprised by guests himself. Or his wife to her surprise might have overdone her usual insistence that she "had nothing to wear."

One day, however, I found myself dumbfounded when a Moroccan guest of honor on the following day justified his no-show by simply explaining that he "hadn't felt at all hungry." Arguably, the sincerest of all possible excuses.

My wife and I would always accept invitations, whether they were extended by a cabinet minister or one of my drivers, a Royal princess or our maid. The Prophet himself advised as much, and once even accepted an invitation by a slave. He would tolerate only two reasons for declining: first, if the host would have to incur debts; and second, if the invitation seemed motivated by pretentiousness. Consequently, I did not think twice about repeatedly turning down wedding invitations whenever it became obvious that the father of the bride merely intended to use an ambassador as a prop to adorn his luxury show.

*

Like all other aspects of life, Islam also governs table manners, that which we commonly call "etiquette."[34] A lot of this will ring familiar, because it meets a certain standard of manners and propriety accepted around the world. Other features are specifically Muslim in tradition and go back to specific directions and actions of the Prophet himself.

In some Arab homes it is customary to envelop the arriving guest in scent from glimmering sandalwood. The guest helpfully opens his coat and fans this aromatic smoke toward him.

One looks for a place to sit as "low" as possible, accepting a seat of honor only when the host strongly insists.

Before serving the meal, the guests are given the opportunity to wash their hands, because that is what they eat with. Especially in Morocco, many hosts turn this into a pretty ceremony. Before and after each meal, a bowl with soap is passed around, warm water is poured over both hands, and towels are offered. On his way out, one sprinkles the guest's hands with fragrance from slender vials of rose or orange water. Upon leaving, many Muslims take out a kind of wooden toothbrush (siwāk) in order to clean their teeth, again following the Prophet's example. It is a twig of soft wood, a little over half an inch thick, which when chewed produces frayed out,

---

34. The fundamentals of Muslim table manners and eating habits are found in the Qur'an (see 5:3-5, 90 f.; 6:145 f.; 7:31; 16:66-69; 24:61; 33:53; 80:24-32), and also in the collected reports of sayings and actions of the Prophet (hadith). The latter can be found in Sahih al Bukhari, translated by M.M. Khan, 9 vols., 3rd edition (Chicago 1977): vol. VII, book 65 (About Eating) and book 69 (About Drinking); furthermore in Sahih Muslim, translated by Abdul Hamid Siddiqi, 4 vols. (Lahore 1980): vol. III, above all in the 21st book, hadiths no. 5037, 5039f., 5097ff., and 5121 ff.

Worth mentioning is also Abu Hamid al Ghazali, Ihya 'Ulum al Din, translated by Maulana Fazul ul-Karim (Lahore, n.d.): vol. 3, book 3, chapter 2 and 3; also Hans Kindermann, Über die guten Sitten beim Essen und Trinken - das ist das 11. Buch von al-Ghazalis Hauptwerk (Leiden 1964); J. Ostrup, Orientalische Höflichkeit, Formen und Formeln im Islam (Leipzig 1929). The refinement and decadence in the court of the Abbasid caliphs can be seen in Ibn al Wassa, Das Buch des buntbestickten Kleides, translated by Dieter Bellmann (Leipzig 1984): above all part II, chapter 29 "Welche Manieren Leute von feiner Lebensart beim Essen beachten müssen" and chapter 30 "Über das Benehmen der Leute von feiner Lebensart beim Trinken."

brush-like tips. I bought one of these in Madinah. The advantage is that one can make do without water and toothpaste.

To allow eating with one's hand, without a knife, food in the Muslim world is cut up in little morsels, which makes other utensils unnecessary. Nowadays, however, knife and fork are offered almost everywhere, not just spoons for the soup (formerly drunk from a cup). Tradition disallows, however, genuine silverware, not just because it takes out of circulation valuable material for minting, but also because it betrays an un-Islamic sense of luxury. (Muslim ambassadors, especially from the Gulf region, whose residences usually brim with precious materials should periodically be reminded of that.)

*

When food is served, the guests help themselves to those pieces of meat, sweets or fruit which are close at hand. It is very much frowned upon to swivel the trays in order to get the more delicious fare. Hosts and dinner partners usually make sure that one's plate is filled with delicacies. Many a time, I found my objections ignored and my plate heaped with lip-smacking treats like lamb's eyes and testicles of ram!

One eats with three fingers of the right hand: thumb, index and middle finger. To use two fingers only is considered haughty, using them all as greedy.

If one does not like a food item, it is all right to pass on it. Muhammad himself did so. He disliked an overbearing amount of garlic in his food. For my part, I strongly dislike cumin, an oriental variety of caraway seeds. Alas, this very spice plays a dominant role in the entire Orient.

Skipping an entire dish is quite easy when the entire course—from appetizer to dessert—is served at once. I witnessed this practice, where the entire table seems to sag under the weight of all too numerous plates, when attending lunches hosted in Bahrain and Abu Dhabi by the emir of the United Arab Emirates, Shaykh Zayed Āl Nahyan, and also during a luncheon given by the Saudi King Fahd in Mina, already described. I cannot help it, seeing bananas and cream tarts next to grilled liver, chicken in almond and lamb chops do not whet my appetite, on the contrary. Therefore, in such cases I limit myself to a couple of dates, a roll, and a banana, bow to the host and leave.

73

To leave right after finishing one's meal would be an insult according to our table manners, for we have been told from childhood on not to leave the table without mom's or dad's permission. Islamic etiquette is different. The Muslim host begins eating first (thereby demonstrating to the guests that the food is indeed safe) and is last to stop. This way, as in Mina, even a king will be the last person at his table.[35]

About my lunches in Mina, Abu Dhabi, and Manama it might be expected that even while not eating very much, I would have at least enjoyed good table conversations. True, but that is not the Muslim way of thinking. Guests in Muslim homes have extensive conversations *before* the meal, talk little *while* eating, and excuse themselves shortly afterwards. This rule allows the host to determine almost exactly how long his guests will stay. In the West, guests staying on interminably and can become a pain in the neck.

Mentioning sagging tables, was not meant to imply that extravagance, above all wasting of food, is the Islamic way—on the contrary. Yes, Muslim hosts from Marrakesh to Dubai and Sharjah view it as a duty to lavish their guests with delectables. At the same time, there is always a whole army of servants and poor people ready to polish off whatever is left over. Nothing goes to waste.

The absolutely overwhelming hospitality shown in the Muslim world presents a real problem for European and American civil servants visiting the Orient on business, because the budgetary rules and regulations imposed by affluent Western democracies do not permit even senior officials —Federal Presidents, ministers, or members of parliament alike—to return such boundless favors in kind. But it is not just the inspector general's office that is preventing us from doing so. We are also victims of a creeping process leading to provincialism, bureaucratization, and a new proletarianism considered "chique." All of which causes us in the Occident to lose the ability to celebrate, represent, and receive with grace, style, and allure. During the April, 1994, GATT-conferences[36] in Marrakesh it was for poor Morocco to demonstrate to the assembled representatives of the entire financial world what it means to be a host in the Islamic tradition. Many a Western official would leave, hanging his head in shame, after

35.   In this regard the Moroccan court protocol does not follow the Sunnah, but Western tradition.
36.   General Agreement on Trade and Tariffs, forerunner of the World Trade Organization (WTO) founded on that occasion.

being sumptuously entertained by crown prince Sidi Muhammad in a tent lavishly decked out, with fireworks and *fantasia* to boot.

*

After discussing *how* the Muslim world eats, let us now describe *what* people eat. Muslim cooking is much like Islamic art: In spite of its enormous variety it is immediately recognizable. This variety was created when each ethnic group, joining Islam—from Mauritania to Baluchistan—contributed its national dish. In the season of pilgrimage, Makkah is the ideal melting pot for an Islamic *cuisine*.

Its common denominator results from the predominance of Turkish cooking, which next to Chinese and French is one of the three *hautes cuisines* of the world. As a matter of fact, different kinds of ethnic food, like the Egyptian, Syrian, and Lebanese way of cooking, can be distinguished by how authentically the Turkish tradition lives on in each of them.

What all of these different kitchens have in common is the Turkish custom of beginning a meal with a variety of cold or lightly warmed, easily digestible appetizers (*meze,* Arab. *mazza,* which means "small snack"): vegetables, greens, fruit, melons, some liver, brain, yogurt, filled vine leaves, red beans, cucumber salad, and so on—much more original and rich than French *crudités*. Collecting their recipes (most require a lot of hand work in the kitchen), my wife discovered that the Muslim world knows many more appetizers than main dishes.[37]

At the courts of sultans, caliphs, and emirs, it was the custom for the entire meal to be rendered more healthful by serving a fruit sherbet in between the main courses of fish or meat.[38]

---

37. These efforts produced an Islamic cookbook, Bülben Hofmann, *Islamische Küche - 150 Kochrezepte aus Maghreb, Maschrek und der Türkei*, to be published soon by SKD-Verlag, Munich, and Cagûri Yayinlari, Istanbul.

38. German Field Marshal Helmuth von Moltke had witnessed these and other eating habits and described them in precise detail when he was military adviser of the Ottoman Sultan. See H. von Moltke, *Unter dem Halbmond - Erlebnisse in der alten Türkei 1835-1839* (Tübingen 1979), pp. 85, 105, 136, 160, 162, 181, 216, 227, 273, 292.

In the Arab world today, things look quite different: guests are being stuffed with meat, fish, and meat again—under the assumption that meat would normally be absent from their diet, for being too expensive.

It is widely known that Islam is not a vegetarian religion. It seems less widely known, however, that Muslims are prohibited from eating meat from animals that have not been expressly slaughtered in the name of God and by cutting the carotid artery, allowing them to bleed out. This is practiced by Muslims all over the world and also prescribed by Judaism. Animals were found to suffer no more from this method than from being killed in discouraging assembly-line slaughterhouses by bolt guns, electrocution, suffocation with CO_2 gas, in allegedly more humane ways.

According to Islamic law, an animal intended for consumption must only be slaughtered lying down, and with a razor-sharp knife. In order to spare it any emotional anguish, it has to be fed well until the very end. It is also not to witness the killing of other animals. Even the sharpening of the blade has to take place behind its back. With one swift cut, the skilled butcher severs throat, gullet, the jugular and the carotid. The animal is thus instantly rendered unconscious and painlessly bleeds to death.[39]

The tiny Jewish community in Germany is allowed to slaughter according to the identical Jewish method. Muslims, however, are cynically prohibited from doing so, because in extreme situations the Qur'an - as makes eminent sense - exceptionally allows food normally forbidden:

if a person is forced by necessity . . . your Lord is Forgiving, Merciful. (6:145)

German authorities bend this into the following "logical" pretzel: If we forbid Muslims ritual slaughter, they will be forced to eat "normal" meat. In that case, their law allows them to consume that meat. Naturally, this sophistry does not quite add up, since with "necessity" the Qur'an refers to a situation of impending starvation. Thus, legalese hypocrisy forces Western Muslims in Germany and elsewhere into a semi-vegetarian lifestyle—or compels them to shop from kosher butchers, which drives logic into circular overdrive.

The Qur'an warns against using religious pretexts for forbidding additional items of food.

---

39. For details see Anis Mohamed Karodia, "Die islamische Methode des Schlachtens," *Al-Islam* no. 2–4 (1990).

Journey to Makkah

Say: Who has forbidden the beautiful things from Allah, which He has
provided for His servants? (7:32)

The Qur'an even recommends specific food items like milk, dates, veg-
etable oil, grapes, and honey, the latter being referred to as a "healing" sub-
stance (16:69). In consequence, honey is used for almost all of the sweet
dishes in the Islamic world, take *baklava*, for instance, this delicious, sticky
concoction of filo dough, nuts, pistachios, and thinned honey.

My favorite "Muslim" dishes are quickly listed. In hot countries one
wants and has to drink a lot—up to two gallons a day—especially someone
like me who for more than twenty years has had to live with only one kidney. That is why beverages are the first thing to come to my mind: almond
milk, cinnamon and ginger water, Turkish coffee, green tea with fresh peppermint, Arabian coffee. It is acceptable—if not recommended as a com-
pliment to the host—to slurp loudly while sipping hot treats. Every hotel
lobby in the east-Arab hemisphere serves Arab coffee, hardly roasted and
thus of greenish color, prepared on charcoal with rose water and a thread of
saffron, and poured over a twig of cardamom into tiny, nutshell-size cups.
One drinks no more than three of these nutshells; One feels reinvigorated
already after the first cup.

Novices that we were in 1982, after a restaurant meal in Makkah, we
ordered "a pot of coffee," as Germans do when enjoying filtered coffee. At
first, we attributed it to the language barrier when the waiter kept coming
back to make sure that a Yemenite jug is really what we were asking for.
Eventually, he relented and brought us one of those characteristically bul-
bous and wide-spouted Yemenite cans filled up with *Arab* coffee. All we
could do with that was take small sips, because after consuming as little as
half a German-size cup, our hearts began to pound and race at record speed.

However, a culinary high point for us to remember without shame would
always be the ceremonial preparation of green tee with peppermint leaves
which is typical of the Maghrib region. I recall with special delight one that
took place in 1989 in the palm garden of the Mozabite oasis El-Ateuf in
southern Algeria. I had given a lecture about "Ten things I do not like about
the Islamic world" at the neighboring oasis Beni Izguen, and afterwards
spent a solitary night in a palm grove cabin.

For breakfast, my host showed up with an entire battery of kettles, cans,
and tea cups. First, he rinsed the teapot out with hot water. Then he proceeded to briefly wash the tea in hot water, which he then discarded. Next,

77

peppermint leaves, a lot of sugar, and boiling water were introduced into this pot. After steeping, there was much pouring back and forth. At long last, everything was good and ready. The host began to fill the glasses with a steady stream from about half a yard above—and did not spill a single drop. Is there a more delicious way to start the morning?

Among my favorite Muslim food items are: stuffed eggplant, lightly browned *(imam bayildi)*, shepherds' salad (with goat cheese), Caucasian chicken (with walnuts), lamb chops *(pirzola)*, humus (puree of chick-peas with sesame paste); Turkish doner kebab; oriental rice, above all Pakistani basmati prepared with pine, cinnamon, and sultanas; salad of cracked wheat with fresh mint *(tabbulah)*; sweet couscous; nutritious *'ashūra'*, *muhallabiyah* (made of rice flour); and the newly invented Egyptian *umm 'Ali* dessert, a heavenly caloric bomb consisting of nuts, milk, and raisins that are served in fire resistant cups, laced with dough, topped by a blob of whipped cream, with a hint of cinnamon.

*

For a conclusion of this nourishing chapter follows a true anecdote about the day when we came into a luxurious and free meal. On Christmas, 1982, we stayed at the Medinah-Sheraton, which is located outside the city area and accessible to non-Muslims, and thus its clients were predominantly Western businessmen. A Pakistani waiter, one of many around, evidently regarded us as such and on our way to lunch greeted me with a friendly "Happy Christmas, Sir!"

I returned in kind with an equally friendly "Thank you very much. By the way, *al hamdulillah*, we are Muslims." The poor guest worker almost fainted, fearing that he was about to be deported back to his home country. And indeed, it took but a few minutes before the hotel manager appeared in order to tender a formal apology for the "terrible insult" we had suffered by his staff. As small and inadequate restitution he asked us to accept our lunch to be on the house. We emphatically reassured him that we had not been insulted at all, that as a Jewish prophet Jesus was entitled to the same reverence as all the other prophets. And do we not invoke the same blessing when speaking of Jesus as we do when mentioning Muhammad: *"salla-llahu 'alayhi wa salam"* (God, bless him and grant him peace)? All to no avail! So we came to realize that many a Muslim has the same difficulties with the Gospel as many a Christian has with the Old Testament.

FATALISTS WITH A PURPOSE

Many a Western reader hardly ever opens a book on Islam without previously checking index or table of contents for key words like "kismet," "fatalism," "evil eye," and "holy war." I do not wish to disappoint these expectations.

The Turkish usage of the term *kismet* (Arabic: *qismah*) was introduced into Germany not by migrant workers from Turkey, but by a popular 19th century German author of adventure stories taking place in the Orient, Karl May. Its Arabic root, the verb *qasama*, denotes the distributing, giving out, allotting—also of fate—to each and every one of us.

Arabs prefer to describe the same with the participle *maktūb*, which derives from the verb *kataba* (to write) and indicates that everybody's destiny is "written down" in what is allegorically pictured in the Qur'an as a large book.

Whether "allotted" or "inscribed," it is the conviction of all Muslims that nothing happens in this world without the advance knowledge of Allah, the All-Knowing.

Even Christians concede that point readily, but are not so fast to accept the inevitable conclusion that given the above assumption, man's free will is not so free after all. I know many philosophers, Muslims among them, who have thought long and hard about predestination and free will.[40] In view of the history of this idea there is no need to be self conscious about stipulating that it is impossible for us to comprehend how the Just God can punish or reward individuals for actions which He, the Foreknowing, the Merciful, and Almighty, could have, or even should have, prevented. By the same measure our logic fails to determine how man should be able to *originate* a causal chain of events.

Heeding the Prophet's advice, we should not rack our brains over that—we could go to pieces over it—and all for nothing.

---

40. See Murad Hofmann, *Islam: The Alternative* (Beltsville 1997), pp. 49-54.

79

*

As for me, I have experienced so many amazing events in my life that could be classified as "kismet" that in happiness and misfortune alike, I, like all Muslims, may be permitted to feel safe and secure in God's omniscience and omnipotence.

1944

In World War II, at the time of the Allies' strategic air campaign over Germany, I lived in my hometown of Aschaffenburg near Frankfurt, a traffic hub, an industrial center, and a city that served as a garrison to five battalions of the *Wehrmacht*. As such, it had been subject to regular air raids beginning September 1940. After sirens had broken my sleep for over 700 times, I chose to spend the night in a shelter outright, already dressed in my street clothes. I went to school carrying a gas mask and an emergency food ration. Then my highschool took a direct hit: right into the very basement that my class was assigned to use as a shelter. However, I had already left school ahead of time, right after the initial pre-alert. Had I been at school . . .

With school no longer functioning, I made myself useful at home, listening almost continuously to the "Figaro" radio-station which was directing the German air defenses. Aschaffenburg was in a grid square identified by them as "Richard Toni 1". This way I knew exactly if it was really necessary to withdraw into the shelter when the alarm sounded.

On November 21, 1944, 150 to 200 American bombers dropped some 1,000 splinter bombs followed up by firebombs, leaving 64% of the city in ruins. Hundreds of people died, 1,900 houses were completely destroyed, 1,000 more severely damaged. About 12 yards behind our house, a number of so-called chain bombs left a series of deep overlapping craters. If the plane's gunner had pushed the button even a tenth of a second earlier . . .

1945

We had gotten used to the constant thunder of the distant artillery along the Rhine, so much so that we were startled by the sudden silence around us. Patton's people had already begun to surround Aschaffenburg a few hours after crossing the Rhine, and taking the city would have been a cinch. And yet they let themselves be scared off by a few old men from the *Volkssturm*, Hitler's motley last stand people's militia, a handful of Hitler youths playing "Werewolf," and a couple of SS-men who had utterly flipped-out in their mindless loyalty to the *Führer*. The Americans reacted with an excessive use of hardware. We made our escape forward, beyond the battle-lines into no-man's land, since our house had become part of the front line. Together with several neighbors, we spent eleven days and nights in an ancient beer-cellar deep underground. It belonged to a garden-restaurant with the demoralizing name "The Final Blow." Every night my mother would prepare a large pot of bean soup at home which I then had to haul all the way to this beer-cellar, through sporadic mortar fire, yet without spelling a single drop. Along the way I would stop to chat with a lonely warrior who had dug a foxhole for himself and his bazooka near our house.

One night when I came around again, the foxhole had turned into a crater. A Thunderbolt fighter plane had targeted my soldier with a five-hundred pound bomb.[41] If I had chatted with him a bit longer . . .

1950

On Christmas, I missed my train from Schenectady, NY, to New York City due to a blizzard. I wouldn't have reached my destination anyway. The train had a serious accident, derailed and turned over . . .

1951

I have already described the car wreck in Mississippi from which the surgeon had not expected me to survive. When I was healthy enough to travel again, I took a long train trip from Memphis, Tennessee, to Washington, D.C. At times I would read, leaning forward, at times I would just look out of the window. I just happened to assume that position when a rifle shot

---

41. See Alois Stadtmüller, *Aschaffenburg im Zweiten Weltkrieg - Bombenangriffe, Belagerung, Übergabe* (Aschaffenburg 1970).

smashed through the window, only a few inches before me. If I had been reading just then . . .

1954

One Wednesday this year, "by accident" I had been lingering in the halls of Munich University's law department when I noticed a clerk posting a note to the door. The new professor for civil procedure, Rudolf Pohle, announced a seminar in his field. Requirement: at least grade "B" in a tutorial on civil procedure. Applications: Wednesdays from 2 to 3 P.M.

I only had one "B" certificate, "by accident" in civil procedure. One glance at my watch: It was just after 2 P.M. This way I became not only the first student Professor Pohle met in Munich, but also his aid and later on his main assistant.

It was only natural then, that I wrote my doctoral (S.J.D.) thesis on a topic of civil procedure comparing the German and American law in point. This, in turn, provoked a research grant for me at Harvard Law School in Cambridge, Massachusetts in 1959, and earned me their LL.M. If on that Wednesday I had not . . .

1955

"Accidentally," again, examiner of my orals at Munich Law School was the doyen of civil procedure, Professor Leo Rosenberg, a frighteningly demanding legal authority. As academic assistant in this very field, I was naturally much better equipped than the other four candidates when it came to defining what the concept of the matter under litigation means for changes in venue, when the verdict becomes final, the extension of the verdict, and prescription.

1959

One weekend my colleagues at the Harvard Law School invited me to a party near my home. They said that I wouldn't have any trouble finding it, only two blocks in the direction of Harvard Square, near Massachusetts Avenue. The house was described as easy to recognize, a "large white elephant house." I heard party noises coming from a house that looked quite like an elephant to me. However, I soon learnt that I was at the wrong party, and yet they didn't want to let me go, saying that there was no such thing like a "wrong party."

Right they were, because it is there that I met Elizabeth-Ann Griffeth, the women I was going to marry half a year later. Would I have an American son today if I had ended up at the "right party?"

1960-1965

The many various ways that tie my destiny to Algeria have already been related in a previous chapter, "A Philosophical Approach to Islam."

FEBRUARY 1976

The Albertina Museum in Vienna presented a Renaissance ballet by Eva Campianu, with period music provided by the Eduard Melkus Quartet. Bülben Uz, a Turkish harpist who was at that time attending the master class at the local Academy of Music and Arts, was urged to attend. She did not feel like going at all (and consequently came late). I, too, was pressured to go by Kurt Peters, editor of the Cologne magazine "Das Tanzarchiv" (Dance Archives). But I did not feel up to it (and in the end really did not write a review). One year later she and I were married. If one of us had not gone after all, as intended . . .

MARCH 1976

I liked Vienna very much, and every day the negotiations between NATO and the Warsaw Pact on MBFR (*Mutual Balanced Force Reductions*) were like a chess game, fascinating anew every day. Even so, after three and a half years I decided to propose transfer. In January, the director of personnel at the German Foreign Office offered me an ambassadorship in Jeddah, Saudi Arabia. In those days before the oil boom,

Jeddah was considered to be a hardship post of the first degree, without even so much as a dentist around.

My American wife had passed away the year before. Would an unmarried man be able to stand this? Thinking about the job scared me stiff—and that is why I signed up.

On the very same day I underwent a medical examination evaluating my fitness to serve in the tropics, contacted my predecessor, studied the "country file," shopped for tropical clothes. Two weeks later, the Foreign Office's medical department suggested that based on their lab results, I should have my urine checked sometime ("blood cells in the urine").

Had I been more concerned about my health in the past, I would have noticed that each of the previous physicals of that type had yielded the same result. But I hadn't attached any recommendation for a follow-up. This time I arrived at the ambulatory unit of the Vienna University Hospital II in order to rush through the test. My attitude was, "Hurry up, I'm off to Jeddah!" Quite "accidentally," a kidney specialist, Dr. Paul Schmidt, was on duty that day, and he was not going to be in a rush with me. Instead, he embarked on a set of ever more complicated analyses. A week later, on March 23, 1976, my left kidney was removed because of a carcinoma (hypernephrom). The tumor proved so aggressive that without an operation I would not have lived another year.

Half a year later, when I returned to Vienna for a follow-up—stationed not in Jeddah but in Belgrade—the result of my urine test was perplexing: I still had blood cells in the urine, but now only half the number. It dawned upon us that the cancer was found through following up on symptoms *that were none after all*. Had I not volunteered to quit Vienna, had I not been offered a post in the tropics, had I not accepted, had I not gone to the clinic, had I not run into the specialist—this book would not have been written.

Such events of higher or lesser drama prove nothing and explain everything. Nothing on a scientific level, but everything on a personal level. They do not prove anything, because interpreting certain causal chains of events as divine intervention is a thoroughly subjective matter. Do we ever know whether an unusual stroke of luck—kismet!—will bring us certain happiness, and whether an unusual tragedy—kismet!—will cause certain unhappiness?

Nevertheless, the events I have just described explain everything to me. My personal feeling of solace and comfort in God is grounded also in those experiences.

*

This feeling can well lead to fatalism—but it is not supposed to, and it won't, provided a Muslim is clear about the fact that God's wisdom can be understood only in retrospect, if at all. Therefore, He can be fatalistic only about past events. Whatever happened he will have to accept, without tearing out his hair, and without bemoaning those who passed on, like wailing women.

That does not mean, however, that a Muslim is expected to sit idly by in a fatalistic frame of mind and twiddle his thumbs as the future approaches. On the contrary: he is expected to be an active member of a community, "inviting to all that is good, enjoining what is right, and forbidding what is wrong" (3:104), and in the process "competing in doing good works" (3:114). Does this sound like fatalism?

We know this problem from the theories of "Historical Materialism" and "Dialectical Materialism" of those communist days gone by. According to Marx/Engels, whose teaching was strongly oriented toward fatalism, history is driven by inexorable dialectical laws toward its end—the classless society. But neither Lenin, nor Trotsky, nor Stalin, nor the international fifth column activists concluded that they would not have to lift one finger toward the building of Communism.

The Prophet of Islam reduced the issue to a simple formula: Tether your camel and leave the rest to Allah.

During my time in Algeria, I kept this in mind when I decided to carry a weapon. I did not harbor any illusions that my pistol would add another second to my life when my time had come. I was convinced then, as I am now, that a bullet that did not hit me had not been dangerous for me, however close it whizzed by me.

Working as Director for Information for NATO (1983-1987), I was again faced by questions as to the purpose of security and self-defense. Several security sources intimated that I might well share the fate of my collegue von Braunmühl, a high-level foreign service official who was shot dead by terrorists. For some time after the warning, I experienced all well-known facets of personal police protection, which can turn into an ineffective routine or grow into harassment. I had pitied the so-called persons at risk for their loss of personal freedom, and now I had to play along with this security-circus myself.

Since the continuing escalation of firepower had relegated my earlier handgun (Walther 7.65) to the status of a ladies' pistol, a gun instructor from the Belgian anti-terror brigade trained me on a gun much more powerful and much faster, developed by the famous German GSG 9 border police unit, a Heckler & Koch 7M14. Appropriately enough, he taught me to defend myself standing up and lying down, in daylight and darkness, with my left and right hand, and with any kind of ammunition. The intense concentration necessary was taking its toll on me.

At the same time there was the mental strain of analyzing every conceivable contingency in order to do the right thing in an emergency, and that means, when in doubt, to sit it out, never to draw without the intention to shoot, and never to shoot without the intention to hit. But even as my scores were getting better and better, and the bad guys on the target board increasingly needed mending of their vital parts, I had lingering doubts about the point of my efforts. Maybe I'm a fatalist after all—in the negative sense?

*

One cannot talk about fatalism in the Muslim world without addressing the phenomenon of the Evil Eye, whose very existence the Muslims and their Prophet basically do not question. Western physicians instead refer to "non-somatic factors," hippies talk about *bad vibes*, and psychologists prefer to think of *self-fulfilling prophecies*, the idea that predictions of catastrophes can bring about their realization.

Naturally, we observe specific cases of the Evil Eye, primarily in places where people think in those terms. To conclude from that, that everything is sheer imagination would be, however, quite premature and unscientific. One might as well make the equally invalid assumption that in other places people do not notice the Evil Eye because they are blind to that phenomenon.

For example, in Turkey I once witnessed how during the visit of an aunt a particularly beautiful plate in the kitchen suddenly broke into a thousand pieces. Let us say the plate imploded because of structural stress, or maybe changes in temperature or additional vibrations contributed to the effect. But had aunt X., well known for her jealous disposition, not just recently expressed her admiration of this beautiful plate? And did we not fail to utter *"ma sha' Allah"* (nonliterally: May God preserve it)?

The only answer to this problem is trust in God. Unfortunately, Islam did not manage to assure this resoponse in the entire Muslim world. Far too many Muslims evidently still believe magic to be more potent than reciting the Qur'an's two surahs of refuge, especially surah 113 (Al Falaq):

> Say: I seek refuge with the Lord of dawn, from the evil of what He created; from the evil of the darkness when it becomes intense; and from the evil of those who practice witchcraft; and from the evil of the envious when they practice envy.[42]

And worse yet, many Muslims are prone to employing these surahs as if *they* were spells and magical charms, in form of amulets. Even the exclamation *"ma sha' a Allah!,"* which is taken from the Qur'an, can be used in a superstitious way.

It is difficult to imagine the extent to which certain Muslim women are still practicing magic. In the suqs of Moroccan cities one can find shops which exclusively sell ingredients for magical rituals: potions and powders, dried lizards and even tiny dolls that are employed to bewitch certain people or jinx them to cause harm, or to make them fall in love, or keep them in love. The Rif Kabyles—and not just them—are famous for this kind of Black Magic.

In Morocco, my wife was quite powerless against the fact that her servants engaged in mixing and burning certain substances both before and after her harp concerts. Before, in order to shield her hands and instruments from the Evil Eye, and after a successful performance in order to protect her from the "evil of the envious." Care was taken to hide the implements of such efforts from my sight.

Those who turn their noses up at such pursuits should first prove that Westerners are not susceptible to magical solutions for their personal problems, starting with the horoscope and ending with "knocking on wood".

---

42.   See Muhammad Rassoul, *Die beiden Schutz-Suren* (Cologne 1982).

*

So let us assume that a Muslim is categorically forbidden to adopt a passive or fatalistic attitude toward his future: that he is rather committed to
exert himself for the realization of what is good in this world. This "exertion" is the first and foremost meaning of the word *jihad*, which many
would-be Orientalists almost gleefully translate as "Holy War."

There have always been wars fought in the name of Islam, be it for real
or imagined, tactical or strategic defense. Even in this day and age a
Muslim head of state can expect to reap political rewards with his call for
a *jihad*. Somehow the souls begin to hum in a different frequency, the willingness to make personal sacrifices increases, especially since paradise is
promised to those witnesses to the faith who perish in the struggle for
Islam. The inherent political potential of this situation is evident. Saddam
Hussein tried to use it for his ends during the 2nd Gulf War in 1991. For
the same reason the secularist Turkish television speaks of a "witness of the
faith" (*sahit*) when reporting on a civilian or soldier killed in Eastern
Anatolia by the Kurdish separatist movement P.K.K.

Certainly the least fatalistic, in a sense the most activist people are the
supporters of so-called Islamist movements, like the Algerian Font for
Islamic Salvation (FIS), who are working for a political breakthrough of an
orthodox-radical form of Islam in their native countries. Highly committed
as they are, and driven by a remarkable moral vigor, these mostly young,
intellectual, and scientifically trained Muslims rigorously attempt to put the
above-quoted Qur'anic verse (3:104) into action.

Between 1987 and 1990, I witnessed this struggle in Algeria, first hand
and up close. It often started when a son—and not necessarily the oldest
one—began to practice his ideals of Islamic morality in his family, making
his sisters cover themselves the Islamic way. In school, the result was that
there were fewer and fewer girls around who did not wear Muslim dress.
The last girls who held out against this trend were advised by their parents
to adapt in order to preserve their chances to get married to a decent boy.
This endeavor continued in the streets. In Bouzarea, I once saw a young
man spit out in front of a woman without veil, crying *"a'udhu billah!"* (I
seek refuge in God!) as if she was a she-devil. Male students in dormitories
all of a sudden refused to go on living in the same house with women, even
when segregated by floors, or to eat at the cafeteria without a clear physi-

cal separation of men and women. Then they proceeded to police the larger society in the spirit of *jihad*. As young Islamists, they saw themselves surrounded after all by a world which had fallen back into the pre-Islamic times of ignorance (*jāhiliyah*). Therefore, they had set their minds on either re-Islamizing these "neo-pagan" societies in what they believed to be a truly sacred war, or to emulate the Prophet and go into (inner) migration.

Beginning in 1988, young Muslims in Algeria began to cut the cables of parabolic antennas in order to prevent the reception of pornographic tv shows. They did not refer to them as *antennes paraboliques*, but as *antennes diaboliques* (diabolic antennas). Others took to smashing bottles with alcoholic beverages in bars, or shredding oil paintings in antique stores if they featured scantily clad women.

These young people went about their cause with great earnestness and idealism and fought under great personal sacrifice and risk for a better world guided by Islamic principles, free of exploitation, corruption, nepotism, privileges, luxury, prostitution, and drugs. Only one thing they did wrong: They violated the fundamental commandment of Islam which in matters of faith forbids any kind of compulsion (2:256). What they achieved was not public morality but public hypocrisy. Furthermore, they stumbled into the same trap as the Puritans before them. As judge, jury, and executioner, all in one and of their own making, they invariably ended up on a track leading toward a religious sort of fascism.

They overlooked that in an orderly State every person is called upon to "enjoin what is right and forbid what is wrong" in his or her own personal sphere of responsibility only. That applies to the mother and father in their family, the entrepreneur in his business, the dean in his university, and the head of State in his entire country.

While these young reformist Muslims do not represent any danger for Europe, they do for their own governments. From January 19–21, 1993, on invitation by the Egyptian High Islamic Council, I participated in Cairo in a conference which dealt with precisely this question without glosses. The respective ministers for Islamic affairs together with their supreme spiritual dignitaries (*muftis*) arrived from almost all of the Islamic countries. But in this composition they represented the very institutions, mutually sustaining each other, from whom young Muslims have become so completely alienated. One had "forgotten" to invite someone who could and would speak for these young people, in particular, representatives of the Muslim

Brotherhood (*al Ikhwan al Muslimun*). This way, the conference became a part of the problem instead of its solution.

Previous criticism notwithstanding, I wish many a Western society the kind of youth capable of embarking on a similar moral quest (or should I say change of paradigm?)—young, upright people ready for martyrdom, if necessary, in their idealistic opposition to what they see as despotism.

MONEY DEAREST

A Turkish saying states that friendship and money mix like water and oil. So how about faith and finances—do they get along?

You bet. In Islam, paying a tax on wealth and growth (zakah) is one of the five pillars of faith and, hence, an obligatory religious duty.[43] To wit, verse 277 of *Sūrat al Baqarah,* enumerates, in no particular order of priority:

> Those who believe, and do do good works, and establish regular prayer, and pay zakah will have their reward with their Lord . . .

As prayer helps to counteract man's pride, and fasting his passions, so paying zakah helps him overcome his avarice and makes it harder to amass huge amounts of wealth. This is why this 2.5% tax is levied even when property has not yielded any profits. The prohibition of interest, to be discussed below, has the same purpose, insofar as it curbs the formation of passive capital.

In orientalist writings, zakah is translated frequently—and mistakenly— as almsgiving or "alms taxes" (a contradiction in terms). Muslims are expected to be charitable, and alms *(sadaqah)* is part of it. Zakah, on the other hand, is a veritable tax which even a rich Muslim State can accept and forcefully collect in order to comply with the Qur'an's instruction (9:60) to meet the following needs: care for the poor and needy, new Muslims, (stranded) travellers, debtors and prisoners, maintenance of an organized government and defense forces, as well as helping to finance activities in pursuit of "God's cause," i.e., the promotion of Islam.

For Islam, considered *"din wa dawla"* (religion and State), this tax is a structural necessity. When, after Muhammad's death, a number of Arab tribes stopped paying zakah, the 1st caliph, Abu Bakr, quite logically fought them as renegades. Not paying zakat equalled apostasy!

43. See *Zakah,* Schriftenreihe des Islamischen Zentrums München, Nr. 6 (Munich 1978).

What to do as a Muslim in the West? Is the obligation to pay zakah not met by paying normal taxes on wages, salaries, and personal wealth as raised in non-Muslim States? After all, these taxes are used for a number of purposes as foreseen by the Qur'an. On the other hand, if no funds are officially collected for the Islamic community, a Western State fails to satisfy one important goal of zakah: The promotion of Islam.*

As a consequence, I am assessing myself for *sadaqah*, to be given in charity to individual Muslims, or payable to Islamic institutions of my own choice, for the most part in Germany. They go to great lengths to assure that such money serves its intended purpose. As an author, I refused to take royalties from Islamic publishers in Germany, the United States, Algeria, and Morocco, as a contribution "to God's cause."

The ability of hundreds of prayer houses *(masjids)* and Islamic cultural centers in Germany to function proves the willingness of many Muslim guest workers to pay their obligatory zakah quietly without pushing the collection bag around as is customary in Christian churches. A kind of offertory box can be found in mosques. But little baskets normally don't make the round in Europe—in stark contrast to the more aggressive "fund raising" typical for American civic culture. People in Europe pay once or twice a year, but then they give a substantial amount. This allows for a more reliable budgeting than if donations dribble in.

Quite naturally many oil dollars continue to find their way into European mosques and leave behind specific, shall we say donor trails. It is true that if the Islamic community in Germany were to be included in the local system of "church taxation" in the same way as the Jewish and Christian congregations, most financial worries would disappear over night. But other, much larger, mainly political worries would take their place. Problems concerning financial control and the distribution of central funds in a multicultural society.

For this reason, one should be especially proud of the Andalusian Muslims around Professor Abd al-Rahman Medina Molera. With the fiery and polemical Raja (Roger) Garaudy strengthening their backs, in 1994,

---

* The basic difference between zakah and taxes is that taxpayers expect benefits (services) to return to them directly or indirectly for their payment, while no such benefits may be expected in paying zakah. In paying zakah, one is discharging an obligation toward God hoping to receive rewards in the hereafter. *Ed.*

without any outside financial help they succeeded in building the first mosque—after 800 years!—in Cordoba, only about 100 yards from the former Great Mosque, and obtaining the right to call for prayer from its minaret. But that is not all! It is affiliated with the "Islamic University Ibn Rushd in Andalusia" which was established in Cordoba in late August, 1994. To other European Muslims, the independence of their Andalusian brothers and sisters from petro-dollars sets an example to emulate.

*

What then is a Muslim to do to maintain and augment his financial assets while paying zakah?

This is another question related to the problem of "avarice," making us run directly into a twofold Qur'anic prohibition. Muslims, also those living in the capitalist world, are forbidden from using their money for gambling or participating in lotteries in order to reap speculative gains. Nor must they give credit for interest. Muslims are supposed to earn a living through diligence and at their own risk.

Issues related to financial markets are rather complex, which may explain why even the "most Islamic" among the rich countries in this world have little qualms about investing vast amounts in the West for high interest rates, and even charge interest within their own banking system.

This is why in December, 1986, the German speaking Muslims gathered in the city of Aachen for a spirited discussion about the right definition of interest in normative verses of the Qur'an, like 2:275. At that time, I brought up the possibility that since the concept at issue, *riba*, was not clearly defined in the Qur'an or by the Prophet, it could be understood relative to its historical context as *usurious* interest, i.e., as exploitation of a financial crisis. Those who have their sportscar or second car financed by a Bank, for instance, could hardly consider themselves exploited. I also pointed out that in some cases interest on savings barely made up for inflation, and that a person saving for interest incurred opportunity costs, losing profit elsewhere, since he might have found more profitable venues for his money. In self-denial, he thus in effect rendered a financial service deserving of compensation.

Although I am not alone in this approach, the response was negative. The majority of the participants stuck to the orthodox interpretation which holds that the prohibition of interest—no matter how big or small—is but one particular subcategory covered by the overarching proscription of usury.[44]

What then is a Western Muslim to do with his rainy-day fund? Although Dr. Ayub (Axel) Köhler from the German Economy Institute in Cologne has made efforts in this direction, there is still no Islamic financial institution in Germany, nor in most other European countries. This is not really surprising considering that even Pakistan is still facing difficulties as she is endlessly trying to develop an interest-free economy. How does one attract capital for investment without the incentive of interest? How to attract money if it will be used at high entrepreneurial risk? How does one allocate resources without using the ability to pay interest as a measure of productivity? How does a central bank conduct anti-cyclical money market policies without the possibility of adjusting interest rates?

At any rate, it is no solution for a Western Muslim to ask his bank for an interest free savings account; indeed, such a proposal would rock the system. In the tried and true tradition of a dedicated civil servant, the teller's response would surely be: "Number one, we've *never* done this before. Number two, we've *always* done it in a different way. And number three, Who do you think you are, anyway?!"

This *attempted* solution, incidentally, demonstrates that one cannot Islamize an entire economic system simply by eliminating interest. The abolition of interest is only feasible as part of a much more comprehensive replacement of capitalism as an inveterate system of limited liability.[45]

Even with an interest-free savings account the problem remains that its owner would willy nilly help his bank to issue interest bearing loans. How hard it is for a bank to get used to customers with Islamic ideas is documented in the kinds of letters I regularly receive from my bank: "Dear Dr. Hofmann, your checking account is currently showing a considerable bal-

---

44.   Ghanie Ghaussy in an exemplary way problematizes interest-free banking in *Das Wirtschaftsdenken im Islam* (Stuttgart 1986), pp. 66; also see Syed Nawab Naqvi, *Ethics and Economics* (Leicester 1981); Umer Chapra, *Islam and Economic Development* (Islamabad 1994); *Elimination of Riba from the Economy*, Institute of Policy Studies (Islamabad 1994).

45.   For a general discussion of an Islamic economy, see Khurshid Ahmad in Ibrahim Abu-Rabi, ed, *Islamic Resurgence* (Islamabad 1995), and Umer Chapra, *Islam and the Economic Challenge* (Leicester/Herndon/Nairobi 1992).

ance. We should like to take the liberty to draw your attention to a variety of attractive investment possibilities . . ."

A Muslim who wants to rule out any risk of violating the Qur'anic prohibition of interest and speculation, even in ambiguous cases, should stay away from fixed-rate investments such as treasuries, as well as from speculative dealings, such as trading in futures, derivatives, or stock market *speculation*—the pure possession of stocks or investment fund certificates as a longer-term investment being allowed.

What is encouraged is to put one's money to work as productive risk capital, as active or silent partner of a commercial company with *personal* liability (Ltd.), or as an investor (not as speculator) in stocks and mutual funds. No financial market is likely to collapse from such restrictions.

*

Fighting greed is also at the heart of the Qur'anic demand to sacrifice animals on the Feast of Sacrifice and other occasions. The Qur'an gives instructions on how to proceed and brings the essential to the point:

> It is not their meat nor their blood that reaches Allah, it is your piety that reaches Him. (22:37)

In Istanbul in 1982 I saw for the first time how a lamb was sacrificed, in the middle of the sidewalk, for the "grand opening" of a shoe store in Beşiktaş. I felt exceedingly uncomfortable watching it. Even after witnessing dozens of similar animal sacrifice, they still disturb me to this very day—as well they should.

The Feast of Sacrifice described in the opening chapter is the main occasion for the slaughter of lambs and the high concluding point of the *hajj* pilgrimage. In Rabat, on that day, the entire nation is waiting for King Hassan II to be the first to discharge his sacrificial duty. Together with the other Muslim ambassadors I joined the king for ritual prayer at the Āl al-Fahs Mosque on the palace grounds. Afterwards, Hassan personally sacrificed two beautiful white lambs, shielded from spraying blood by a white cloth. Shortly after, at home I had to attend the ritual slaughter of two more animals, performed by my cook and surrounded by his large, festively dressed family. One of the two lambs he had bought himself, the other one, our "royal lamb," was an annual gift from the king. While I could delegate the slaughter and skinning, I still had to be present in order to exclaim "bismillah" and pray over the animal. And only a few hours later we were already eating our share of the sacrificial meat, a good size helping of skewered liver. The rest was dutifully given away in large portions to embassy staff and our numerous housekeepers.

Most frequently, births serve as an occasion for further sacrifices. According to local custom which follows after the prophetic tradition, a lamb is sacrificed in order to give thanks to Allah for the newly born member of the family.

Sheep markets shortly before the Feast of Sacrifice are something special. In 1994, when traveling from Sebta (Ceuta) to Rabat, in front of the gates of Tetuan we found ourselves among thousands of bleating lambs, each one surrounded by haggling fathers with their sons. The mood was festive. But everything was blocked by the strangest vehicles designed to haul off sheep. It took us as much as one and a half hours to inch our car across from one end of this buzzing market to the next.

Another customary event that called for a sacrifice of thanks was our successful move into a newly renovated residence in Istanbul. The most convenient facilities to this end are located near the Eyüp Sultan Mosque on the upper Golden Horn. One pays, personally chooses the lamb, gives instructions on what is to be done with the meat, and attends the animal's ritual slaughter.

People in the West have managed to banish, at least visually, from everyday life the disagreeable facts surrounding birth, aging, disease and death. Nothing with blood on it is to disturb our tender sensibilities. A woman giving birth disappears in the delivery room and emerges to show her family her made-up face. In modern clinics, the sick are turned into hotel guests; old people are disposed of in nursing homes—not even the word "old" can be allowed to disturb us! And when it comes to dying, people find themselves under wraps in a "terminal home"—what a cynical euphemism.

And the animals—I almost forgot all about them—are slaughtered *en masse*, and we do not see it, smell it, or hear it. They arrive, packaged as breasts or legs, in clean and sterile, shrink-wrapped portions deposited in the freezer and ready for the microwave.

A world like this quite naturally "feels" that the sacrifice of living beings is barbaric, and senseless to boot. Yet to this day, churchgoers talk about mass as a mystic *sacrifice*, and on Good Friday continue to meditate on how God *sacrificed* his very son—not only an animal—on the cross for us.

Indeed, animal sacrifice is a question of life and death . An animal will lose its life sooner or later, just as we lose our life sooner or later. The difference is whether the inevitable loss takes place as a conscious gesture before God, or—if you will—as a miserable, wretched death.

Remember, it is not meat nor blood that reaches God, but the grateful devotion of the sacrificing individual. Those who don't understand can't be helped.

CHERCHEZ LA MUSLIMAH!

The rhetorical suggestion to look for a woman behind everything—
cherchez la femme!—applies to the Muslim world as well. If it is true that,
as they say, there is a woman behind every successful Western man, then
there is a *Muslimah* behind every successful Muslim. No slave, but a
beloved partner. Ergo: *Cherchez la muslima* !

First, a few preliminary generalities before embarking on a detailed
report on the "State of the Women in Islam":

1. Muslim women and their Western sisters have much more in common than
   is generally assumed in Europe or the United States. In both worlds, women
   appear as wives, mothers, lovers, artists—actresses, singers, dancers -,
   politicians, journalists, poets, physicians and nurses, grandmothers,
   matrons, slaves, witches, mystics, saints, and much more.

2. In Occident and Orient alike, most women pursue their happiness in a sup-
   plementary relationship to men, perfecting each other through complemen-
   tation, and not through imitation.

3. As in many other respects, here, too, is a sizable gap between the Islamic
   ideal and Muslim practice concerning the rights of women as provided in
   the Qur'an.

4. Even though there are those marginalized, mediatized and fully cloaked
   women in the Islamic world; the vast majority of my Muslim sisters do not
   recognize themselves in books such as "Not without My Daughter," or "A
   Princess from the House of Al Saud."

*

And now on to the particulars,[46] beginning with marriage. In Muslim
countries, women are hardly ever married against their will—but it does

---

46. About the rights of women in Islam, see Hofmann, *Islam the Alternative*, p.
163–185.

happen. Frequently, they do not have sufficient opportunity to find a partner on their own because the local customs do not permit it. As a consequence, to this day many marriages are arranged by the parents, as is the case from Pakistan to eastern Anatolia, and from Morocco to Mauritania.

In theses parts of the world one simply assumes that the parents' choice, based on a lifetime of experience, is no worse a bet for a happy marriage than a union bound by what unexperienced youngsters call love. In fact, arranged marriages are no less stable than love marriages. Of course, stability is a reliable statistical indicator only where wives are financially independent enough to leave their husband if they wanted.

Prospective brides are mainly discovered by prospective mothers-in-law. For that no place is better suited for that than the *hammam*, the Turkish bath, where no one wears bathing suits. There, a young girl cannot disguise or hide any physical imperfections, but on the other hand a *hammam* provides her with a golden opportunity to meet in peace and quiet and an intimate athmosphere with a large number of potential mothers-in-law. In any event, parents or guardians make sure that a traditional Muslim marriage be based on a carefully drafted *marriage contract,* one which could exclude a second wife and provides for a big dowry to give the bride a measure of financial security in case of divorce. An ingenious method to stabilize the marriage is a codicil which stipulates that the dowry only comes due, at least partly, in the event of divorce. Just as is the case in American and German law, such proviso in financial terms renders divorce a potentially prohibitive financial risk for the husband.

The amount asked for as dowry can get so far out of hand that many young men in countries like Saudi Arabia are forced to find cheaper wives abroad, preferably in Turkey or Egypt. Saudi women seem to have become downright unaffordable except for the affluent. The option of "shopping" for wives abroad is closed in the United Arab Emirates (UAE). Because of the extraordinary threat of an overbearing foreign influence this country's sons are only permitted to marry the country's daughters. In order to make this financially feasible, the Emir of Abu Dhabi has been subsidizing each of these marriages to the tune of what in 1993 amounted to $50,000.

This problem already existed in the days of the second Caliph. Indeed, 'Umar wanted to put a reasonable ceiling on what might be demanded as dowry. But he canceled these plans after being publicly rebuked in the mosque by a woman who convincingly argued that the Qur'an (4:20) even permitted whole "treasures" as dowry!

Islam views marriage not as a sacrament, but as a (noncommercial) contract. Many times, however, the signing of the contract and the consumption of marriage are one to two years apart. In Morocco, we had been invited to both: a ceremony celebrating the public conclusion of this very important contract, and the "real" wedding much later.

In 1977, I got married the Islamic way in Istanbul, with a German document certifying my marriageability as a basis for the preceding Turkish civil ceremony. The ceremony with a *hoça* was modest and essentially limited to admonitions and prayers. A big dowry was unnecessary, since the marriage made my wife eligible for pension benefits on the federal German payroll.

In the Islamic world, weddings are and always have been quite lavish an affair, with the ceremony varying from region to region. However, based on Islamic laws governing the family, they all have certain features in common. For instance, there is the custom everywhere that men and women on the eve of marriage meet for separate celebrations ("henna evening"); during their weddings, Muslim brides receive valuable (gold) jewelry as a provision for old age. (Favoring women, a strict separation of the spouses' respective properties had been established by Islamic law 1400 years ago.) In Turkey, I am at times worried that the bride could be dragged down to the ground under the combined weight of all the gold chains, gold rings, and golden watches with which she becomes increasingly draped during the gift ceremony.

From Turkey to Morocco, another common feature these days is the unfortunate trend toward ever louder electronic noise. Nowadays, when large weddings are held in major Istanbul hotels, the concomitant fireworks will rattle the entire city. In Morocco, this nuisance has reached utterly absurd proportions. For the last fifteen years, weddings there have become a veritable acoustic torture, for the participants as well as for those innocent residents who are in the unfortunate situation of living within a two-mile radius of the event. "Sleep for no one when my daughter gets married" seems to be the motto.

The festive ruckus is such that conversations at the table are rendered impossible. Even on the day after one feels half deaf. For the next wedding in Morocco, I was seriously determined to don the earguards left over from my target practice.

The Maghrib has a custom that is described by Sheherezade in the 22nd night of her famous narrative: in the course of the wedding celebration, the bride presents herself to the guests in a succession of seven different dresses plus accessories, representing the colorful costumes from the different folkloristic regions of the kingdom. The last dress nowadays looks like a European wedding gown.

Especially in Morocco, it is the custom to carry the bride like India's Muslims do: swaying her back and forth on the shoulders of stout matrons while she is sitting in a cage fashioned from silver wire or wicker. The husband, too, has his grand entrance, announced and accompanied by dark-skinned musicians from Marrakesh who completely without electric amplification unleash an infernal noise with their two-yard long trumpets, resounding drums, and metal castanets.

The couple spend the entire night sitting on a throne, facing the guests, and without any kind of speech or eye contact between them. This puritanism is what the good old-fashioned and buttoned-up society of inner Anatolia also demands. Things are a little bit more humane in Turkey's cities. Here, bride and groom at first sit facing the guests as well, but they are allowed to speak with each other and in the course of the evening will also mingle with the guests.

We have participated in such weddings—always elaborate production pieces with identical ceremonies, identical menu and (nonalcoholic) beverages—among privileged as well as "little people," as guests of my chauffeur Hajj Muhammad Jniha in Salé and of our petite, illegal tour guide Idris in Fez, as well as at classy weddings of ministers' daughters in Rabat. There was one big difference though: the simpler the people, the more cordial the hosts, and the merrier the event.

*

Few things stimulate the sexual fantasies of Europeans and Americans more than when they enviously conjure up steamy pictures of debauchery in an Oriental harem. If they know but one thing about Islam, it is this: Muslims, those lechers, have *four wives*. Thinking about it, they are likely

102

to start drooling. And yet: even this spotty knowledge is false and divorced from reality.

It is *false*, because the Qur'an permits polygeny only where children who have lost a parent need to be provided for. And even this humanitarian exception is contingent on a condition which is virtually impossible to fulfill psychologically: to deal justly with more than one wife (4:3, 129).

It does not reflect *reality*, because *the Muslim world is in practice no less monogamous than the West*. Statistically, Muslim monogamous marriages are considerably more stable than the average American, Swedish, or German marriage.

Although I have lived and traveled extensively in the Islam-Arabian world, I remember only very few cases of polygeny. Oddly enough, in Rabat's Souissi district resided an Egyptian businessman married to four *German* women! And those four seemed more content than the female members of Fritz Teufel's large commune, formed by Germany's patriarchal anarchist of the late sixties. One can observe in Istanbul, too, the occasional polygenous Anatolian *agha* or the equally rare Arab shaykh who with his two, three wives is seeking refuge from the heat of the Arabian peninsula in the Tarabaya Hotel. The ones who profit most from this phenomenon are the bazaar's merchants in jewelry and watches. To comply with the Qur'anic command for equal treatment, such a husband either has to give each of his women the same item—or give nothing to any.

In Abu Dhabi, in December of 1993, I watched another case of polygeny that did not seem to be sanctioned by the Qur'an. A young Emirati appeared for lunch at the seafood restaurant at the lagoon of the Hotel Intercontinental with four younger women of about the same age (and who looked very much alike) as well as four kids almost identical in age.

Not to mention one of my fellow ambassadors from sub-Saharan Africa, who had one wife with him in Rabat and another one at home, quite like the proverbial mariner with "a bride in every harbor."

Finally, I should mention Maryam Jameelah, an American Jewish intellectual who converted to Islam. Seeking to emulate the wives of the Prophet, she actively sought out a polygenous relationship in Pakistan. There she now consciously lives in the tradition of those "Mothers of the Believers."

This short but exhaustive list of my encounters with polygeny shows that in accordance with the Qur'an it does no longer, on the whole, present a problem for Islam. If as a Muslim I was allowed to bet, I'd wager that there exist more firmly established mistresses in the West than second wives in the Muslim world.

*

Westerners are convinced that things tend to get quite ugly in Islamic marriages. Everybody believes for a fact that *Muslimah*s are battered and virtually enslaved.

As far as I can see, most women in the Muslim world lead a fulfilled life with their husband, fulfilled also in terms of her sexuality. (Female circumcision—a mutilation of women—is, thank God, is a rare custom which has nothing whatsoever to do with Islam. It is true, on the other hand, that a certain "paternalist" spirit distinguishes many Muslim marriages. Her husband and her brothers take the *protection* of a Muslim woman so seriously that it can result in a limitation of her personal freedom, not only from the point of view of women's liberation. Evidently, the honor of the family is crucial here. In fact, more than any proprietary instinct, the family's sense of honor seems to foster an attitude that we tend to misread as mere jealousy. Upon close scrutiny, male chauvinism, too, has very little to do with this phenomenon. On the contrary: most Muslim men try to protect their wives from getting into precarious situations so they do *not* have to get into a brawl with somebody whom she might have "turned on," possibly by being (un-)dressed in a provocative fashion.

A girl's *virginity,* as a family asset to be protected by father and brothers, continues to play a major role in the Muslim world of mores. In certain areas, such as among the Turkish Kurds, it still happens regularly that "fallen" girls are expelled and even killed for disgracing the family. In any case, loss of virginity reduces the chances of landing a (profitable) match. No wonder that certains surgeons profit from their ability to skillfully fix up all kinds of calamities.

But even the *protection* of women can be taken a little too far. Thus Moroccan women in spite of owning a passport are prevented from leaving the country if they cannot produce a travel permit signed by their husbands.

The phenomenon of imposing one's protection on a woman even when she herself does not see the need, has its roots in the prefatory sentence of a Qur'anic verse which men for centuries now have interpreted as a sign of genetic or statutory male superiority.

In several reputable German translations of the Qur'an—as well as in many English and French renditions, verse 34 of the surah 4, *al Nisā*, opens as follows:[47]

Men are superior to women. (M. Savary)

Men have precedence before women. (Pesle/Tidjani)

Men are the managers of women (Hamidullah)

Men have authority over women. (Boubakeur, Masson and official Saudi translations)

Men are entitled to be in charge of women. (Mazigh)

Men have responsibility over women. (Rassoul)

Men rank higher than women. (Goldschmidt)

Men rank above women. (Paret)

Men are superior to women. (Henning)

Men take responsibility for the women. (M. Ali)

All of the above renditions of the passages in question (my translations) draw the conclusion that the husband is his wife's boss. Thank goodness, the Arabic text—*"al rijāl qawwamuna 'ala al nisā'"*—does not convey that meaning. Translated straightforwardly and without male chauvinism, these four words simply mean: The men assume responsibility for the women.

As the rest of the Qur'anic passage reveals, this is so because on balance men usually are physically and financially stronger and thus *responsible* for

---

47. I consulted the following Qur'an translations: Muhammad Ali, *Der Heilige Qur-an* (Zurich 1954); Yusuf Ali, *The Meaning of the Holy Qur'an*, 6th edition (Beltville, 1995); Muhammad Asad, *The Message of the Qur'an* (Gibraltar 1980); Jacques Berque, *Le Coran* (Paris 1990); Hamza Boubakeur, *Le Coran*, 3rd. edition (Paris 1985); Lazarus Goldschmidt, *Der Koran* (Wiesbaden 1993); Muhammad Hamidullah, *Le Saint Coran*, 13th edition (Brentwood 1985); Max Henning, *Der Koran* (Leipzig 1901); Adel Khoury, *Der Koran* (Gütersloh 1987); Denise Masson, *le Coran* (Paris 1967); Denise Masson and Sobhi El Saleh, *Essai d'interprétation du Coran Inimitable* (Cairo and Beirut, 1980); Sadok Mazigh, *Le Coran* (Paris 1985); Rudi Paret, *Der Koran* (Stuttgart 1979); O. Pesle/Ahmed Tidjani, *Le Coran* (Paris 1980); Muhammad Ahmad Rassoul, *Al-Qur'an al-Karim*, 7th edition (Cologne 1995); Author Collective, *Le Saint Coran*, (Madinah n.d.); M. Savary, *le Koran* (Paris 1893).

their wives. If *she* is the financially or physically stronger one, he must not impose his protection on her.

This is not the only known case where men have adapted their understanding of the Qur'an to their prevailing habits, rather than adjusting their attitudes to the norms of the Qur'an, which are much more favorable to women's interests than usually admitted from the male side.

This was first brought to my attention by Abdullah Borek, the former chairman of the German Muslim League, Inc. (*Deutsche Muslim Liga, e.V.*), and by the Egyptian scholar Fathi Osman. Luckily I am, however, not alone in calling for a reappraisal of the Qur'anic passage in question. English speaking authors have been reevaluating 4:31 already for quite some time:

Men shall take full care of women. (Asad)

Men are the ones who should support the women. (Irving)

The men are the protectors and maintainers of women. (Y. Ali)

The men are to provide for the women. (Berque)

The men have power of attorney and are responsible for the women. (Khoury)

Out, therefore, with the outdated notion a superior genetic status enjoyed by men.

There is a case, however, where a woman can certainly not do without male protection: the pilgrimage. On pilgrimage, she must under all circumstances be accompanied by a *muḥrim*, a (in terms of marriage) "forbidden" male chaperon. He does not have to be her husband, but can be a brother or her father—provided they are Muslims. On this score, Saudi officials are repeatedly faced with a most intractable problem, because the 20th century comes up with situations the 7th century hardly knew: single, converted Muslim women wanting to perform the hajj without any other Muslim in the family. Year after year it happended that German *Muslimahs* who have found their way to Islam all by themselves could not go on a hajj for lack of a *muḥrim*. (Once, in the case of an 80-year-old, newly converted widow, the Saudi embassy in Bonn decided to look the other way.) Of course there is always the possibility of entering into a fictitious Islamic marriage concluded simply for hajj purposes and for the duration of the pilgrimage. Yet even this would mean violating the occidental law which normally does not allow even fictitious church weddings without prior civil ceremony.

Despite—or perhaps because of—the above mentioned protection of women—which can of course be maligned as structural violence—Muslim family life as a rule is not any less peaceful than non-Muslim family life. Women, especially the husband's mother, are often quite vocal and frequently have the last word. Henpecked husbands are a global phenomenon.

It certainly happens that women get beaten, especially by drunken men, but this definitely does not occur more often in Islamic regions than in the West. Violence in the family does not have any authentic "Islamic" roots, just as Christianity can hardly be held responsible for battered women taking refuge in safehouses.

I feel somewhat sorry when destroying this prejudice, too, because I know how nice it is to claim the moral high ground. But does psychological need really justify using Islam as a whipping boy?

*

If one measures a woman's opportunity to fully realize her own potential by her chances of participating in professional life, things look up in many Muslim countries. Literacy campaigns for girls are gradually being advanced everywhere, often against the resistance of short sighted families. In countries like Algeria, Egypt, Morocco, Lebanon, Syria, Tunisia and Turkey, the percentage of women with higher education is substantial, as compared to Saudi Arabia, Yemen, Sudan, Mauretania, and the Gulf states. Female doctors, lawyers, journalists, authors, and university professors are as numerous in Turkey as they are in Egypt or Morocco. These countries, as well as the Emirates, have opened their armed forces to women. In their memo dated March 1994, even the Egyptian Muslim Brotherhood is supporting the active *and* passive female suffrage, thereby affirming a woman's role in political life.

Therefore, it is quite consistent with the Islamic system of values when Muslim countries in the persons of Tansu Ciller and Benazir Bhutto already pioneered what the emancipated United States of America has yet to produce: a female head of government.

But just like in Europe, there is a conspicuous lack of female representation in the ranks of parliament, and this is so because also Muslim women tend not to vote for other women. They are thus perpetuating their own traditional roles in the political arena. (In 1993, the Moroccan voters only elected two women to the National Assembly; before that there had not been a single woman in the Moroccan parliament).

A judge's seat, however, is likely to present a bigger hurdle to climb—except for juvenile courts. The reason is that from an Islamic, a Jewish, a Catholic or an Orthodox point of view, any activity relating to the administration of the faith is exclusively set aside for males. In Islam, this applies to the functions of head of state, imam, *mu'adhdhin*, and also *qāḍī* (or mufti), i.e., judges. No use waiting for a change. Women as Islamic equivalents to female Christian pastors or bishops—that will never happen.

Not everywhere can Muslim women play a role in public life. As is well known, women in Saudi Arabia are not allowed to drive cars or work as television announcers. At Saudi universities, female students follow lectures by male professors via closed-circuit tv monitors.

The policy of veiling women away from public view is not to be equated with the harmless separation of the sexes that occurs after leaving the table during mixed dinner parties in the Muslim and also the British world. When men retreat to one drawing room (Turkish *selamlik*) and women gather in another (*haremlik*), they are not motivated by a sense of religious duty but simple practical reasons. There are quite a few things men and women are eager to talk about which may be of little interest to the other sex.

With all this I do not mean to condone the practice of people like the Ibadite Mozabites in southern Algeria who treat and keep women like children whose interests in addition to men and love, are reduced to six topics: kitchen, kids, clothes, jewels, religion, and health. During a conversation, I was pointedly asking some highly educated Mozabites how an intelligent man could be satisfied with a naive nymphet for his wife, and I was amazed at the sad response: "Well, after all, one doesn't spend much time with one's wife, or does one?"

Behind some people's rigorous separation of the sexes one finds an excessive exegesis of certain normative Qur'anic verses, such as the so-called verse of the veil (*ayat al hijab*, 24:31; see also 33:53,59). A correct reading confirms that parts of these regulations do not apply to Muslim women in general, but only to those of the Prophet; in any case, they neither demand a total separation of the sexes, nor the complete cloaking of Muslim women from head to toe, face included.[48]

---

48.   See Hofmann, *Islam the Alternative*, p. 178.

Given ambiguous doctrinal and unequal cultural background conditions, it is not surprising that Muslim women do not act uniformly as far as their requisite "outer garments," their "Islamic dress" is concerned. *Muslimah*s from Indonesia, Pakistan, Anatolia and southern Algeria, for instance, dress quite distinctly from each other. What a variety in unity!

In this regard, there are two very visible lines separating the Muslim world. One distinguishes women who cover their hair from those who do not. In Morocco, the aunt of the ruling monarch consented to a request from King Mohammed V in the 1950s to remove her headdress. Since this demonstrative revolution it has become more or less customary for women in Morocco to show their hair. The same goes for the major cities in Algeria, Egypt, Jordan, Syria and Turkey, where women with open hair dominate the streets.

The second line distinguishes women who cover their hair from those who also cover their face. Although without solid foundation in the Qur'an, the *facial veil* is still around in a number of Muslim countries. This is odd because even on her pilgrimage a *Muslimah must not* cover her face! The veil can be seen occasionally in Marrakesh, as well as in Cairo, Istanbul, Dubai or Ghardaia, but seems to be gradually disappearing.

In 1982, my wife and I traveled in Saudi Arabia on our "little pilgrimage" ('umrah). Upon conclusion of the rites of pilgrimage, she had to veil her face with black gauze, four-fold. She found that quite practical—except for becoming a traffic risk—because she could leave the house anytime, on moment's notice, without make-up and hairdo. (Many western women appreciate a head scarf and dark shades).

Ever since the Gulf War the picture in Saudi Arabia has, however, begun to change. The traditionally unveiled wives of Kuwaiti refugees who were pouring into Jeddah by the thousands have arguably caused a sea change. In general, women there do not wear veils any more; in Riyadh, most still do.

Those who wish to see exotic or extremely elaborate veils must travel to northern Yemen, where some women still wear face masks made of leather, or to the southern Algerian M'Zab, where women only leave *one* eye uncovered. But even that obviously does not afford enough protection: Whenever they encounter a man in the alleys of El-Ateuf or Beni Izguen, they turn away toward a wall.

It would be wrong to conclude from such observations that the modest, neck-high and loose Islamic habit plus headscarf which Muslim women wear in Europe and America is forced on them by jealous husbands. Those women who dress the Islamic way do this in obedience to God and in order to be recognized and respected as women of dignity.

German *Muslimah*s illustrate that view very well. A great number of them found their way to Islam all by themselves, without a Muslim husband, and as the only one in their family. In public, and when looking for jobs they sometimes suffer discrimination or, as a minimum, are teased because of their dress. At best they are shrugged off as a deplorable curiosity. However, their Muslim dress also has an advantage. It serves as a visible token of their Muslim identity and thus as a conversation starter about Islam. They are happy to speak freely about their faith and are relieved that their clothes so demonstrably remove them from the erotic marketplace.

While most of my German sisters liked my book *Islam: The Alternative* (Beltsville 1997), many were put off by one particular point: my opinion that covering a woman's hair is necessary only in societies where its display had an erotic effect on men of that civilization (p. 132). In July, 1993, a group of German Muslim women called me on the carpet at the House of Islam in Lützelbach so that I could hear their disappointment first hand— and in all friendliness.

Be that as it may. I hope that readers won't find it difficult to agree with me that there is more to Islam than the issue of properly covering women's hair.

*

In the Muslim world, too, there is "what must not be": children born out of wedlock. The reason for that is not that Islam would in any way frown upon *birth control*—prophylactics, that is. As a matter of fact, many preachers in the mosque actually advocate systematic birth control and appeal to the believers' sense of social responsibility in the face of the ongoing population explosion. But most of the listeners (for whom—in the absence of effective social insurance—children are still a form of old age insurance) obviously say to themselves, "Just let the imam talk!"

In the Catholic Church it is the same in reverse. Here, too, many of the faithful obviously say to themselves: "Just let him talk!" when their priest lashes out *against* birth control.

Islam, however, forbids any kind of interference when a child, out of wedlock or not, is already on its way. The majority view among Islamic scholars is that *abortion*, the killing of a defenseless person, is a crime against life. The minority view, which holds that abortion is permissible until the end of the fourth month, is fast losing support as became evident during the Conference on World Population in Cairo in September 1994.

Illegitimate children are foreseen by Islamic law and may, therefore, end up without name and claim. Islamic law rejects *adoption*. Therefore, things can look very grim for an illegitimate child unless the family sweeps the situation under the rug and accepts the baby into the family, instead of abandoning it. The parents, even a mother not married to the father, cannot forsake their parental rights once and for all. Therefore, an illegitimate child can only be given into the care of contractual foster parents which can be terminated by the biological parents at any time. As a result, an abandoned child will find foster parents most easily if his real parents are completely unknown.

The ruling that adoption does not establish legally valid family ties has its source in the Qur'an: Muhammad had been given permission to marry a woman, Zaynab, who had been unhappily married to his "adopted son" (This would have constituted a legal impediment in case of a real son.)

From the Islamic point of view adopted children in the West invariably suffer great distress, followed by trauma, when they finally learn—which is inevitable—that they are not their parents' natural offspring. Add to this that adoption contracts necessarily disadvantage a (nonconsenting) third party: him or her who in terms of inheritance would have been the beneficiary but for the adopted child. Finally, adoption is unacceptable as a man-made interference into a genealogy which should be respected as a God-given destiny.

Childless couples from Germany, Italy, and France, who are traveling to the Maghrib on the lookout for an orphan, could not care less about all of this. Without the slightest pangs of conscience, they even become pro-forma-Muslims for a few hours, only to get their hands on a baby. German courts dealing with matters of guardianship do not have any problem either when "interpreting" an unambiguous Islamic foster care contract into a valid adoption contract, even as they know that this would have been null and void in the country of the child's origin. Using their concern for the "welfare of the child" as a justification for bending international private law, magistrates in the end allow themselves to dismiss Islamic law outright in order to finalize any otherwise illegal adoption of foreign born Muslim children. The process does not seem to burden the judges' conscience. "An Islamic legal system?" they seem to say, "That must be something barbaric. Does it not serve the "welfare" of any child to snatch it from the clutches of Islam?"

There is a fitting term for this attitude: cultural imperialism.

*

A *divorce* in Islam—as now also in the Occident—does not require an extramarital affair. It is frequently sufficient for its pronouncement that a woman is unfortunate enough to be childless—or not to bear a son. Although a Muslim *is not supposed* to, he is nevertheless *allowed* to legally dissolve the marriage without compelling or even stated reasons, and that by unilateral declaration *(talaq)*. The fact that a husband has to pronounce such a divorce three times for it to become valid, and that on different days, is not much of a consolation for a wife "dumped" that way.

I met even very high ranking Muslim wives who were living in constant fear of waking up one morning to learn—possibly by a mere representative of their absent husband—that they are not married anymore. (In a recent reform of Moroccan family law in 1993, the kingdom did away with the option of pronouncing a divorce by a go-between. They could do this, because the Qur'an did not establish such a practice.)

Yet, of all Islamic legal provisions, it is the one allowing the dissolution of a marriage by one partner and without a compelling reason toward which progressive Western jurisprudence in America and in Europe has been gradually moving. According to articles 1565 ff. of the German Civil Code, just moving out is nowadays sufficient even in Germany if one party to the marriage rejects the "matrimonial ties" (§ 1567 BGB), even though the waiting period for the dissolution of the marriage of a seperated couple takes a bit longer than under Islamic law. 365 days instead of at least 3. Thus Western law systems now belatedly acknowledge the rationale of the institution of *talaq*: That a successful divorce is better than a desperately broken marriage, and that families are better suited for setting marriage trouble than State institutions and courts of justice.

When the divorce is initiated by the wife, Islamic law requires that a judge decide; while the unilateral dissolution of the marriage by the husband (*talaq*) only needs to be officially recorded after the fact. This difference is due to the modalities of financial support. A man who divorces his wife cannot get one penny of his dowry back, even if his wife provoked the divorce. If wives could dissolve their marriage all by themselves, without intervention of a judge, this could be a possible incentive to get married in succession, for financial reasons only, each time a divorcing shortly thereafter. Aside from grave physical defects, there is only one compelling case for divorce: If a Muslim's wife, be she Muslim, Christian or Jewish, becomes atheist. This once happened to a Bosnian Muslim, whom I met at a Muslim gathering in Aachen, Germany. His Croat wife had just left the Catholic Church because she had lost her faith in God. As a consequence, she had also lost her husband.

Christian and Jewish wives of Muslims risk other disadvantages: Should their Muslim husbands pass away, according to Islamic law, non-Muslims cannot become legal heirs of Muslim estates. In the case of a divorce, non-Muslim women are not entitled to continue raising their children, since they should grow up in a Muslim environment; of cource, the divorced parents can arrange among themselves for visits of, or by, the children.

Who knows how many Christian wives of Muslim men have joined Islam for these two reasons alone? Thank God, many of them have, however, become true believers after experiencing the cordiality and coherence of Islamic families. Others have remained Muslims of convenience, and they readily admit to that.

So far, I have not learnt of a divorce for reasons of *homosexuality*. In fact, sociological and socio-anthropological studies have shown that homosexual activities in the Muslim world are usually of a temporary nature, sooner or later terminating with normal bi-sexual marriage relationships. Such behavior cannot escape attention, given that entering marriage is a basic religious obligation for either sex in Islam.

Although the Qur'an through recounting the story of Lūt disapproves of homosexuality, if only for economic reasons it does play some role in the

Muslim world as well. It is indeed no exaggeration to state that one would have to travel all the way to San Francisco California in order to find a degree of tolerance of homosexuality similar to what exists in Morocco.

It was for a good reason that many homo- and bisexual American artists of the Beat Generation, like Tennessee Williams, Truman Capote and William Burroughs, flocked to the international zone of Tangiers, and that some—like Charles and Jane Bowles—decided to stick around. To this very day, Tangiers is a magnet for homosexual sex tourists. And yet, while Islam commands to show compassion for all fellow men, it will never condone homosexuality as an optional "life style" or "orientation" or conclude homosexual "marriages."

*

At the end of this chapter, the reader is probably left to wonder how all of the above reflects on the *emancipation* of Muslim women in general. There is no easy answer, especially since the conditions vary considerably from country to country. In any event, one should not be deceived by "poster"-feminists like Fatima Mernissi who reap tremendous accolades abroad and indifference at home, as she does in her native Morocco.

There is no need for the *Muslimah* to emancipate herself as far as her status before God is concerned. In this regard she is entirely on an equal footing with men. She is to fulfill all the obligations of a Muslim—praying, fasting, taxes and pilgrimage—and just like him she and her partner can aspire to a blissful life after death in God's presence.

In terms of human rights and the civil code, the *Muslimah* is essentially equal to men as well; above all, her husband has no access to her private property. Marriage does not make her lose her maiden name. According to Islamic law, she retains it all her life—without hyphenation. Ironically, this prerogative may cause her problems when crossing borders: Border policemen do not readily understand why her legitimate child, traveling with her, does not carry the name of his mother.

There also exist legal differences between men and women which the *Muslimah* does not take as discrimination, because they are based on factual differences.

114

That she inherits less than her brother is not in contradiction of equality under the law, because it is he alone who will have to bear the financial burden of supporting the entire family, not she. She also agrees with the reasonable Islamic distribution of educational tasks in the family. She has the last word with the little kids, he with the bigger ones.

Against this background, the entire issue of emancipation boils down to the question of whether Muslim women have a fighting chance to compete successfully in traditionally male dominated professions (outside the religious administration). The answer is: I do not know.

I cannot know it, since most Muslim women are not seeking their happiness in the total emulation of, and assimilation to, men. Just like most European and American women, they usually do not want to become streetcar operators, cab drivers, fighter jet pilots, or combat officers, but rather prefer to cultivate their primary and central role as focal point of the family. The reason for this rather traditional orientation is not a lack of a "politically correct gender consciousness," but rather the realization that many paragons of emancipated Western womanhood have come to regret by now that they had rejected family and/or motherhood and thus fell way short of the true measure of their existential femininity. In short, the competitive chances of the *Muslimah* are hard to gauge, because she is intent on a career *as a woman* who fully endorses the God given male-female polarity, even as she deploys her female advantages (not "weapons") to achieve her feminine ends.

To sum it up with a provocation: When I tell my wife about the exploits of one or the other feminist heroine, she usually responds with a malicious inquiry: "Is she pretty?"

HUMANITY ICE COLD

Why, of all places, had it to be Istanbul for me? Is it not true that each year, this city of 12 million inhabitants already is destination of 500,000 further immigrants from Anatolia, Bosnia, Bulgaria, Macedonia, and Albania, a number which is higher than the total combined number of asylum seekers and settlers of German descent moving into all of Germany in 1992? Indeed. But in Turkey this influx neither precipitates constitutional and governmental crises, nor does it trigger civil war in Istanbul.

Is it not true that air pollution rates there of up to 1000 mg carbon dioxide per cubic meter are high enough in winter to make throat and eyes burn?—True. And what about attacks perpetrated by Kurdish separatists?—It happens. And runaway inflation?—Ditto. Islamic parties, periodically outlawed, gain more and more votes?—So what. Almost every day, there is the odd black out, and faucet water comes every third night only?—Correct! An impossible city indeed.

And yet, all of this counts for nothing. For Istanbul is situated in breathtakingly beautiful surroundings, a bustling, vibrant city replete with rich, seemingly indestructible architectural monuments going back over 1700 years. Neither Hongkong nor San Francisco, Stockholm, Copenhagen, Paris, Rome, or Lisbon can rival Istanbul. Lest we forget: Until quite recently, this was the seat of the 400-year Ottoman Caliphate (1517–1924). But that is not all: Istanbul is a *warm* city, even when the temperature outside dips below freezing, because the locals support and warm each other with their irrepressible humaneness. People here are very effusive with each other—or very hostile—but never merely "formal" or just correct. Neighbors in apartment housing are either friend or foe, but never—as is so often the case in Western agglomerations—indifferent or even unknown to each other. When someone dies, the neighbors know well before any odor serves notice. (New Yorkers know what I mean.)

As a people, the Turks are the epitome of sociability. In fact, they think of themselves as basically one large extended family. Indeed, blood lines

117

are honored, almost going all the way back to Adam and Eve. Family ties are cherished into the nth-generation.

We benefited from this at a time when I was posted in Belgrade, while my wife was still working in Istanbul as a harpist for the opera and symphony orchestras, and as a teacher at the conservatory for classical Turkish music. The train ride to Belgrade via Bulgaria took about 27 hours. When I was worried that my wife should spend the night on the train alone by herself, she responded with a smile: "You are forgetting again that brothers and sisters of mine are everywhere." I reminded her that those countrymen were highly unlikely to travel First Class.

Nevertheless, my wife was right. It was always the same: Passing by, a Turkish guest worker would poke his head into her compartment, look at her closely and say: "Sister, if you need food—or assistance—you'll find me in the next car."—Solidarity.

Vibrant life? In our part of town it is not just the call of the *mu'adhdhin* we hear, but dozens of street vendors with their resounding voices and their own characteristic tunes. Shopping here is a pleasure for my wife. It makes her feel like a princess, more so than being *Madame l'Ambassadrice"* ever could. No merchant keeps her waiting or would have her carry home a kilo of grapes, no matter if she shops Saturday night or Sunday morning. (Within three minutes, a little boy delivers the order to the door for a small tip or *bakshish*.) Recently she ran into her butcher on his way home. He spontaneously offered to open his store again if she required anything.

In 1980, we had been looking for some Pakistani basmati rice *(cilav)* at our little corner grocery in Teşvikiye. It is the most delicious rice there is, but that day—because of foreign exchange problems—basmati could not be found in the store, nor anywhere else in the city. Even the Egyptian Bazar was blank. Three months later, in our Bonn residence, we received a call from a Turkish person we had never met before. He introduced himself as the friend of a friend of our trusty grocer. In short: He was to deliver to us four pounds of basmati rice. When could he come by?—Always ready to help.

Instead of those grumpy, prying Parisian *"concièrges"* lurking in their dark dens, janitors in Turkish cities have wives who with their colorful dresses sit in front of their houses, on the sidewalk, chatting busily among lots of playing children, exactly as they used to do in their Anatolian villages. Human warmth.

My wife would love shopping for the simple reason alone that there is price transparency, not just in the bazaar. Walking, we can reach within minutes seven hairdressers, seven grocery stores, six banks, four butchers, and seven appliance stores. Nobody has the slightest chance to get away with manipulating exchange rates, higher prices, or inferior merchandise. Superior service alone recommends a business.

On July 22, 1980, in the covered bazaar (Kapali Çarşi) of Istanbul, I was able to observe first hand how brotherliness can temper business competition and give it a human face. We were standing at a shop window, looking with interest over a display of souvenirs, unaware that the shop was unattended at the moment. Noticing this, the owner of the souvenir shop next door came over and started to praise the wares of his competitor. To act that way seemed quite natural for him, instead of trying to lure us over into his neighboring place. What a contrast to *"cut throat competition"* among American businessmen!

I was equally amazed when I took a cab home from Istanbul airport on October 2, 1995. The cab's meter showed an amount somewhat higher than usual for this trip. After I had paid, the driver returned some of the money: It seemed to him that the meter was not working right.—Brotherliness.

The bazaar-principle of price transparency even extends to the wedding business. In the remote city district of Bagûcilar, there is a street exclusively lined with "wedding-saloons," hairdressers, and boutiques selling wedding dresses and accessories. On several floors, weddings take place simultaneously. No, people here don't segregate, neither in sadness nor in happiness. (In fact, it is quite natural for family and friends to come together in the home of a deceased person, fourty days after his death, to pray for his soul.)

We chanced upon the strangest wedding bazaar because fairly distant and fairly poor relatives had invited us to a wedding celebration there. We were invited because, after all, kinship obliges in the Muslim world. We agreed to come, because in the Muslim world one does not turn down wedding invitations, even if one has to put up with a 90-minute cab ride and afterwards has to clamber up seven floors of a tenement without elevators, with an 80-year-old mother-in-law in tow. Family sense.

*

Against this background it is understandable that my wife is shivering from the cooling of human relations in Germany, even in the heat of summer. We are not the only ones who feel that way. It was for precisely this reason that former State Minister Hans Jürgen Wischnewski ("Ben Wisch") declared on German TV on October 16, 1994, that he had been "distressed for several years now because solidarity among Germans today was poorer than ever before." During a convention of his Christian Democratic Union (CDU) on October 16, 1995 in Karlsruhe, even Chancellor Helmut Kohl warned of a "cold, inhumane, unbearable" atmosphere which resulted when "people are so preoccupied with communications technology that they stop talking to each other".

This is a well-known phenomenon: In Germany (almost) everything functions with an (almost) noiseless, (almost) incorruptible and exemplary efficiency in administration, production, transportation, communication, healthcare and welfare. We are not only a nation of law and order; nothing escapes regulation, even the sorting of garbage.

In this disciplined, programmed, productivity-oriented, routine-driven and boring society, there is but one uncontrollable and disruptive risk-factor: man. But he is engineered to be as aseptic and dispensable as possible by way of digitalization and automatization of all walks of life. Woe therefore to the irksome individual who, defying routine, gets caught in the web of a conflict with administration, police and courts of law. The relationship of the citizen to the bureaucracies which claim jurisdiction over him are based more on the strictness of positive law than on equity and fairness, hardship clauses notwithstanding. Therefore, the struggle of an individual against the "system" can become downright kafkaesque. Hardship clauses do not replace hard hearts. The Romans coined a fitting phrase for that phenomenon: *"Summum ius, summa iniuria"* (Justice driven to extremes begets extreme injustice).

What I am describing with some hyperbole is a creeping process, in part formed by a tendency toward selfish isolation. To be a Turk is to be *many;* to be German is to be *single.* Grandparents are separated from their grandchildren and shipped off to nursing homes. What is more, even men are considered an optional accessory by those women who aim and choose to become single mothers. Does anybody know how the American,

120

Scandinavian, and German people 30 years hence are to cope with a generation of children who have been deliberately excluded from the experience and influence of a father and deprived of real family life?

In the Islamic world, too, public servants are subject to laws and are scared of the inspector general . And yet, in that part of the world there is always hope that hardship cases will be resolved in a humanitarian spirit and generosity, even if this implies a breach of regulations. This, and only this is what I mean when suggesting that the harshness of Oriental laws can be "alleviated by corruption." There is a harmless example for that phenomenon, too: After the prayer for the dead at the Selimiye Mosque in Kadiköy in August of 1994, we drove to Cengelköy cemetery where the funeral was scheduled. We were driving on the Asian side of Istanbul—less well known to us—and therefore, in mid-traffic missed the last exit before the highway bridge across the Bosporus. We stopped at the toll booth and asked the police to allow us, and assist us with a U-turn on the highway, otherwise we would miss our funeral.

You know what is coming: We made it to the grave on time. What would the German *autobahn*—police have said in that situation? Probably nothing. Because we would not even have dared to ask.

Compared to that, many Western "humanitarian" missions ring hollow to me, and much Western "humanitarian" engagement sounds like mere chatter. I cannot quite get over the feeling that much of that primarily serves as an alleviation of the West's guilty conscience. During the war in Bosnia, would it not have been more humane to help the Muslims defend themselves by lifting the arms embargo, rather than just making sure through "humanitarian aid" that they did not have to face their enemy on an empty stomach—in a word: to protect them from starvation, but not from military defeat "ethnic cleansing," and massacres?

I am exaggerating? Certainly, pretty drastically at that, and at once in all directions. Naturally, every description in Manichaean black-and-white has bill-board poster quality. In reality, the world cannot neatly be split into "goodies" and "badies"; nevertheless, the trend toward de-humanization outlined above is very real. It is both part and consequence of what German TV-commentator Ulrich Wickert diagnosed in his book as "The Loss of Values" (1994).

Journey to Makkah

*

Before being accused of glossing over the fact that the acclaimed "humane" behavior on the part of Oriental authorities is merely a symptom of structural corruption, I should like to address this suspicion head on. It is certainly true that in the Orient (most of the world, for that matter) people hold out their hand for every favor done, even when legal claims are satisfied and thus merely justice was done. I remember not a few occasions, though, when Oriental bureaucrats acted against the law without expecting or accepting any "gratuity," out of simple compassion. Apart from that it is a little harsh to brand the acceptance of a tip as "corruption" when the salary of a public servant is so small that he can hardly eke out a living. A functionary who only makes between $140 to $200 per month suspects that his employer quietly assumes that he will bring up his salary through *bakshish*, at least up to the poverty line. In view of that, European businessmen in the Orient consider even exorbitant *bakshish*—also called "commission" or "sponsoring"—as additional taxation which should be tax deductible back home.

*

Why all this theory. The story of my marriage to Bülben Uz, my second wife—a marriage arranged under a tremendous rush—explains this much better. Back then I was posted in Belgrade, where the first follow-up meeting to the Conference for Security and Cooperation in Europe (CSCE) in Helsinki was scheduled to begin on May 3, 1977. I had been notified as deputy chief of the German delegation. We received the indispensable certification of my marriageability from Bonn so late that—if our wedding was to take place at all in the foreseeable future—Monday, May 2, was the only option: the eve of the conference.

When I arrived in Istanbul during the weekend before, Bülben—with a lot of *bakshish* XE "bakshish" —had already arranged for our wedding to take place at the registrar's office in Nişantaş *no later* than 12:15 P.M.! However—there was a catch: On that Monday morning, we first had to have the marriageability certificate officially translated into Turkish; then we had to get the German General Consulate to legalize the translation,

122

Bülben Hofmann, Shaykh al Azhar, and Murad Hofmann, Cairo 1989

with an additional legalization to be obtained from the governor's office of Istanbul province. In addition to that, I had to undergo a test for venereal disease at the German hospital (no gratuities accepted), and, in turn, had to have this lab report, too, legalized by Istanbul's health department. All of this within three official business hours and large distances to cover.

Our chances for success were slim enough, but they grew even dimmer on Sunday, May 1, when bloody political unrest broke out on Taksim square, where some of the government offices relevant to our case were located. It looked like a war zone: torched cars, bloody spots, broken windows. Who would have the courage to show up in his office the next day?

Nevertheless, come Monday morning we were off to hunt down the still missing documents. Being a colleague, the German Consulate General took care of me before regular business hours. But once we got to Istanbul's government offices—on the other side of the Golden Horn—we had to push and prod five inert officials with hefty bribes just to get them moving: one of them recorded our application in a notebook; from the second we purchased a sticker for a fee, which the third one canceled with a stamp, the fourth one double checked everything, the fifth one—two floors above— condescended to sign off. The German hospital, however, drove us to despair. People there calmly insisted that we wait two hours for the lab result to come back. By now, we had become so discouraged that when it came to ordering the wedding announcements, we did not dare to give the printer a concrete wedding date.

With the health certificate finally in hand—it was 11:00 A.M. by then—we rushed onto the health department obstacle course. Twice we had to scamper upstairs to the fifth floor—and down again. Here, again, *bakshish* was able to direct a secretary's attention away from the care of her finger-nails long enough to rouse a clerk to breathe life into a dry stamp. For the short distance from there to the registry—a mere 800 yards—we jumped into a cab.

At long last, at 12:05 P.M., exhausted and sweaty we were standing before the decisive official who, due to numerous interventions by our friends (and their friends), was said to be favorably disposed to "our case." Or was he? Perusing the file, he got repeatedly hung up on discrepancies. Naturally, some important legal waiting periods had not been honored. There had been no public marriage announcement. And there was no interpreter, who is absolutely mandatory when foreigners—as in my case—do not know the language.

At that point, the eyes of my wife-to-be began to fill with tears, and so—with typical male stupidity—I concluded that our attempt had failed. It did not occur to me that there could be tears of joy. What the chief registrar had actually told her was: "Let us do it now—and make it quick! If someone else was in my place you would be waiting for at least another six months!"

This is how we finally exchanged vows, in jeans and sweater, and with the secretaries of the registry in attendance as witnesses. To the ceremonial questions of the administering official I truthfully responded with *evet!* (yes!) or *hayir!* (no!)—not because I understood him, but because my bride gave me signals that we had worked out before.

The rest of the day went by fast. Bülben went to the hairdresser. Her siblings worked the phones to rally guests for a small reception. The wedding night was short. At five A.M. I was on my way to the airport, departure 7:15 A.M. Thanks to the one hour time differential between Turkey and Yugoslavia, the JAT plane arrived in Belgrade also at 7:15. My little Porsche waiting at the airport made sure that I would make it in time to the preparatory meeting of the German delegation at the convention center of Novi Beograd. The ambassador, Dr. Per Fischer, concluded the meeting by asking if someone had anything to add under "miscellaneous". "Yes," said I, "I did a bit of marrying yesterday in Istanbul."

This hair-raising account might suggest to some that the Orient is hopelessly corrupt. Did I not just admit myself that we would not have gotten married without a lot of *bakshish*? (By the way, are we "properly" married?) But this story speaks much louder of something else altogether: It is about bureaucracy with a human face which exists in the Orient, and about people reaching out to each other in a generous, warm-hearted fashion. May this human kindness not altogether disappear from America, Germany, and the Occident as a whole. In this regard, a little Islam could go a long way.

Islam in Germany
. . . A German Islam?

From May, 28 until August, 1989, the Gropiusbau in Berlin hosted a magnificent exhibition entitled "Europe and the Orient 800–1900," which demonstrated the countless Islamic influences on all areas of Occidental Art, from architecture, painting, crafts and music to etiquette, language and fashion.[49]

Compared to that, the *religious* influence of Islam on Europe during this period had been minimal, particularly in Germany, which contrary to Spain, France, and Austria had never suffered Muslim siege or occupation. In the year 732, the Arabs did not penetrate beyond Tours and Poitiers, and the Turks repeatedly tried to bite off more than they could chew at Vienna in 1529 and 1683.

In spite of the fact that there is proof of diplomatic contact between Charlemagne and the Abbasid Caliph Harun al Rashid, genuine bilateral relations between Germany and the Islamic world were not established before 1731 at the earliest. This was the year when the Prussian King Frederick William I recruited twenty Turkish soldiers for his guards. For them, the first mosque in Germany was improvised in Potsdam in 1732. Under his successor Frederick the Great, the number of Muslim soldiers in Prussia's pay—Tatar deserters, Bosnians and Albanians—grew to over 1000, so that an imam (the first one ever in Germany) had to be appointed especially for them. Germany's oldest Muslim cemetery in Berlin also dates back to this time, the second half of the 18th century.[50]

---

49. A catalogue worth having was published by Bertelsmann (Gütersloh 1989).
50. For the earliest history of the Islamic community in Germany, see M.S. Abdullah (Herbert Krawinkel), *Geschichte des Islam in Deutschland*, Graz 1981; *Halbmond unter dem Preußenadler* (Altenberge 1984); and *Ein Abriß der Geschichte der islamischen Minderheit in Deutschland* (Altenberge 1987).

In the 19th century German-Islamic contacts were beginning to strengthen. Captain Helmuth von Moltke served the Osman Sultan well from 1835 to 1839. Another civilian advisor, Dr. Eduard Schnitzer, who became a Muslim and under the name of Mehmet Emin Pasha, launched a remarkable career as governor of Equatorial Egypt. The adventurous German convert Karl Detroit from Brandenburg as Mehmed Ali even became field marshal in the Turkish military.

It was Kaiser Wilhelm II, however, who would "take the cake" in his efforts to be recognized as protector of the Islamic world (in opposition to English, French, and Russian colonial expansion). His highly visible, even spectacular visits to Istanbul in 1895, to Damascus and Jerusalem in 1905, and Tangiers in 1905, have all left their mark. It was no accident that the driving force behind the Young Turks, Enver Pasha, cunningly maneuvered Turkey into World War I on the side of the Central European powers; he had been military attaché in Berlin. During that war, another mosque had to be constructed in the vicinity of Berlin to accommodate the roughly 15,000 Muslim POWs from Russia, North Africa, and Senegal. It was ceremoniously opened in Wünsdorf, near Zossen, in 1915, in the presence of the Turkish ambassador.

A native German Islamic community did, however, not come into evidence until 1922. It gathered around the Indian Maulana Sadr ud-Din, who was able to take possession of a properly domed mosque in Berlin-Wilmersdorf, in 1925.

With World War II came the problem of taking care of and housing about 60,000 Muslim POWs. This problem not only had a different dimension than 1914–1918, but was of a political nature. Incited by the former Grand Mufti of Jerusalem, Amin el-Husseini, residing in Berlin since 1941, many Muslim prisoners of war volunteered to fight alongside the German *Reich* both against the colonial powers and Soviet atheism.[51]

The *Wehrmacht* and the military arm of the SS not only tolerated a "Central Institute of Islam" in Berlin; they did not miss a beat when it came to manipulate Tatars, Turkomans, Kirghiz, Montenegrins, Bosnians or Albanians for their ends. The *Wehrmacht* in 1944 even ran an army school for the training of their own Islamic *mullahs*.

---

51. Klaus Gensicke, *Der Mufti von Jerusalem Amin el-Hussein und die Nationalsozialisten* (Frankfurt 1988).

Journey to Makkah

The Muslim units wore German uniforms with shoulder insignia in Palestine colors showing the inscription "Free Arabia" in both German and Arabic. (Here again Germany posed as "protector" of the Islamic world.) In 1n 1945, this adventure ended suddenly—and for many Muslims tragically. But a German Muslim teenager, Mahmoud Heitmann, did manage after all to escort the Grand Mufti el-Husseini most of his way back to Jerusalem.

In the 19th century, study and research of Islam began to gain a good reputation in Germany as part of Middle Eastern studies. Indeed, to this very day, German orientalism has defended that reputation of nonpartisanship, even in the Islamic world. This is because German scientists—quite in contrast to the British secret agent Lawrence of Arabia—did not promote colonialism. Their approach was rather in tune with the positivist spirit characteristic of the sciences of their times. For instance, Theodor Nöldecke (died 1930) in a monumental effort attempted to date every single verse of the Qur'an, thereby setting a lasting example, also for Islamic researchers. In the 20th century, Rudi Paret, who taught at Tübingen University, dedicated his entire life to the Qur'an, as a worthy heir to a scholarly tradition founded in the previous century.

In the process, the Germans had begun to take a closer look at the Qur'an. itself.[52]

Its first translation into German, by Salomon Schweigger, was published in Nuremberg in 1616. Significantly enough, it was still entitled *"Alcoranus Mahumeticus, das ist: Der Trken Alcoran, Religion und Aberglauben"*. (Muhammad's Qur'an, i.e., the Turks' Alcoran, Religion and Superstition.) Considering the fact that it was not based on the original Arabic text but on an Italian version which, in turn, had been based on a Latin rendition, one can imagine the (fourth-hand) quality. This defect was corrected, at least as far as the method was concerned, when David Friedrich Megerlin translated the Qur'an in 1772 under the title "Die türkische Bibel" (The Turkish Bible) directly from the Arabic.

52. An alphabetized list of all Qur'an translations into German can be found on pp. 213–235 of the 1986 edition of *World Bibliography of Translations of the Meanings of the Holy Qur'an*—Printed Translations 1515–1980, edited by the International Resarch Center for Islamic History, Culture and Arts (IRCICA) in Yildiz-İstanbul. Muhammad Hamidullah provides on pp. LXII–LXV of the introduction to his Qur'an translation *Le Saint Coran* (Brentwood 1985) a chronological list of German Qur'an translations; he even includes sections translated into German dialects.

It was this version which, recommended by Johann Gottfried Herder, brought Johann Wolfgang von Goethe so close to Islam that many people to this very day have been suspecting that in his heart of hearts he had become a Muslim. Although it is well established that Goethe was a confirmed, anti-clerical deist, he did leave behind the following cryptic statement in his own commentary on his collection of orientalist poetry, the *"West-östlicher Diwan"* (West-Eastern Divan): "The poet does not deny the suspicion that he himself was a Muslim".[53] How delighted Goethe would have been if he could have seen the unique attempts of the scholarly orientalist poet Friedrich Rückert to translate the Qur'an into German poetic meter.[54] Take, for example, the ingenious transversification of *Sūrat Al-Iklās* (112):

Sprich: Gott ist Einer,
Ein ewig reiner,
Hat nicht gezeugt,
und ihn gezeugt hat Keiner,
Und nicht ihm gleich ist einer

Qul: Huwa Allahu aḥad,
Allahu-s-samad,
Lam yalid wa lam yulad.
Wa lam yakun
lahu kufu'an ahad

(Say: He is Allah, the One and Only
The Eternal, Absolute;
He begets not,
Nor is He begotten
And there is none like him.)

Since that time, twenty more German translation of the Qur'an have been published. Currently, there are at least six versions available in bookstores, but only three complete ones written by Muslims.[55]

---

53. See the 19-part series "Goethe and Islam" by Ahmad von Denffer in the periodical *Al-Islam* no. 1–4, 1990–94; the quote is printed in no. 4, 1994, p. 28. In *Dichtung und Wahrheit*, Goethe made it clear that he "never considered Muhammad as a fraud." In this, too, he was ahead of his time. See Goethe, *Werke*, vol. 5 (Frankfurt 1993), p. 569.
54. Friedrich Rückert, *Der Koran* (1888), reprint (Heidelberg 1980).
55. There are seven editions already by Muhammad Ahmad Rassoul: an annotated translation by a team of Muslim women published by the Munich SKD Bavaria Verlag, in 5 volumes, pp. 3000 (1996); and two editions of the most recent translation by Ahmad von Denffer (Munich 1996).

Journey to Makkah

*

In terms of frequency and intensity, our times eclipse everything that went before in German-Islamic contacts. Nowadays, Islam is everywhere and not just here and there, as was the case in 1814, when Goethe by chance encountered a group of praying Russian Muslim soldiers from Bashkiristan. Today, about three million Muslims live among the Germans, and the same goes for England and France. Everywhere representative mosques are being built, in Paris, London, Rome, Bonn, Vienna, Zagreb, and even in noncapital cities like Mannheim and Pforzheim.

Europeans from all over the continent, above all women, are converting in ever increasing numbers. In earlier days, this was just a matter of extraordinary individuals, like Muhammad Asad (Leopold Weiss, d. 1992) or the mystic Frithjof Schuon (d. 1998). Today, people from all walks of life are drawn to Islam, be it from popular music (Cat Stevens/Yusuf Islam) or dance (Maurice Béjart), sports (Cassius Clay/Muhammad Ali) and politics (Raja/Roger Garaudy). In Germany, about 60,000 ethnic or second generation Germans profess Islam.

This development raises a number of questions which I intend to pursue below.

Which social classes do most converts come from?
What are their motives?
How are they organized?
What about official recognition of Islam?
What are the problems in terms of schooling, diet, holidays, fasting, mosque building, or funerals?
Can a Muslim really live in Germany?

I suppose that much of the following material while situated in Germany has a bearing on Occidental Muslims no matter where.

*

There are international and German collections of records recounting the different ways Europeans came to Islam, their individual "journeys to Makkah." Lisbeth Rocher and Fatima Cherqaoui according to a set pattern,

131

conducted numerous interviews with European and American Muslims, among them Germans like Arifa Gaspary, Muhammad Aman Hobohm, and Eva El-Shabassy. Their systematic analysis became an intelligent book, *D'une foi l'autre* (From One Faith to the Other).[56]

Compared to that, the small book put together by Muhammad Ahmad Rassoul, *"Deutsche von Allah geleitet"* (Germans Guided by Allah), contains a simple collection of confessional material, such as accounts of their conversions by Frank Abdullah Bubenheim, Hassan Ndayisenga, and Fatima Heeren (Grimm).[57]

Both collections demonstrate that there is no one typical way to Islam but many, very many individual "roads to Makkah." According to Rocher/Cherqaoui, the large majority of today's Western Muslims heed an inner calling, as was the case with their great predecessors, Shaykh René Guénon (1886–1951) and Muhammad Asad (1900–1992), conversion being the result of a maturation process.

And yet: Most German converts can be divided into four somewhat overlapping groups. To keep it simple, I shall call them "guest workers," "spouses," "greens," and "islamologists."

Guest workers in this context are not Tunisians working in Germany, but Germans who work in Tunisia or other Muslim countries and during their sojourn found their way to Islam. There are engineers among them, architects, construction workers, as well as all kinds of experts in all kinds of trades whom the Society for Technical Cooperation (GTZ) sends all over the world, and members of German foreign missions and of their military attaché staffs.

The group of *spouses* consists of Germans who fell in love with Muslim women and had to become Muslims in order to marry them. Many a man took Islam as a trade for his wife; but Allah has his own ways of guiding people to Islam.

The group called the *greens* consists mostly of young people who have been protesting the excesses of modern industrial society by taking the social emergency exit. Many of them pursue an ideological quest for a universal brotherly society that is more just, has higher moral standards and lacks restrictive hierarchies: a society that warms and nurtures, provides

---

56. Ed. Seuil (Paris 1986).
57. Verlag Islamische Bibliothek (Cologne 1982).

clear orientation and invests a life that has lost all meaning with a deeper, even profound *raison d'être*. One obvious reason why the Islamic community in Germany is particularly attractive to converts is its internationalist athmosphere—thanks to Muslims of all races from the third world—of which they are so fond.

At times the journey to Islam is marked by the most peculiar detours. Characteristic stops could include a socialist commune, a flirt with Buddhism, or being the disciple of some Baghwan-guru. Sooner or later, for many of such people in transit, Islam becomes the final destination.

The last group, the *islamologists*, chiefly comprises students at any of the 19 German universities offering classes on Islam. These people have embarked on an academic career in Oriental Studies because they feel an unexplained affinity to the Arabo-Islamic world. To them, their academic education becomes much more: the emergence of something which up to this point had been but an oblique and nascent calling.

Many of the new Muslims, quietly and almost imperceptibly, grow into Islam. The prominent French *Muslimah* Eva de Vitray-Meyérovitch described the process correctly as follows: "One does not convert to Islam, one rather embraces a religion which contains all the other ones."[58]

*

The fact that most German Muslims have come to Islam via close contact with an Arab country, Turkey or Pakistan is sometimes quite glaringly obvious, because many converts develop an overbearing orientophilia manifested in their dress. In order to emulate in detail even the outer appearance of the Prophet, they like wearing billowing *jallabiyah*, sometimes even a turban. And in sprinkling their German with Arabisms, they are acting, as Ahmed Schmiede observed, like "cultural parasites."[59]

It is understandable that a new Muslim intends to show the infidel (*kafir*) world around him that he has undergone a profound change. He also wants to be recognizable to other Muslims as a Muslim brother. And yet, dressing and eating like an Arab from the Hijaz of the 7th century while being

---

58. Quoted from Lisbeth Rocher/Fatima Cherqaoui, *D'une fois l'autre* (Paris 1986), p. 20.
59. Ahmad von Denffer (ed.), *Islam hier und heute* (Cologne 1981), pp. 73ff.

a German in 20th century central Europe is rather questionable; since it is a sure way of becoming "a stranger in one's own land" (Abdullah Borek) and of projecting Islam as a subculture, even as mere religious folklore.

This effect is detrimental, especially since many Muslims in Germany who are guest workers already run the risk of slipping into an urban backyard ghetto. That is not where Islam belongs! As an underground religion it may survive in a dictatorship, but not in a democracy.

This is what simmers behind the debate among German Muslims: about "What is the German Muslim's fatherland?" Should he, must he emigrate like the Prophet in 620 from a godless into a godfearing world? If, however, he is really at home here, and Germany is his fatherland, why not dress like a German? (Better still if he wears his beard like the prophet.)

Abdullah Borek, himself living in Manama (Bahrain), sparked a fruitful discussion about this with his memorandum "Zur Lage der deutschen Muslims" (On the State of the German Muslim) presented at the 42nd gathering of German speaking Muslims on June 8, 1991 in Lützelbach.[60] He sounded a timely warning against portraying to Germany the world religion of Islam with its (now) 1.3 billion followers as a mere appendix of Turkish politics and culture. (Or else we might foment the very prejudice of which the Qur'an-translators Schweigger and Megerlin had already been victims in the 17th and 18th centuries!).

Borek added that in Germany Islam had to be represented by German—not naturalized but German born—Muslims so it cannot be dismissed any longer as a religion. He reminded us that in its history, Islam successively assimilated the most diverse traditions, to wit the Arab, Iranian, Berber, Nubian, West Gothic, Indian, Indonesian, and Turkish civilizations. Why not, therefore, Islam with a European face? (Or an American, British, French "smell"?)

Borek's speech was controversial in two ways, even though his basic assumptions were right: Why should Islam not assume a European shading, as long as this does not amount to a revisionist "Euro-Islam" threatening the integrity and unity of faith? Methodically, American and European Muslims have much to offer Islam thanks to their uncensored scientific curiosity and skepticism. They do not only bring fresh blood into Islam, but also new visions. They were not raised in the authoritarian athmosphere

---

60.   The text was published in full in the periodical *Al-Islam*, (Munich 1991), no. 2.

endemic to education in Muslim countries. Consequently, they are better predisposed, if not qualified to throw open the long bolted door leading to a more relevant understanding and contemporary interpretation of the inalterable foundations and sources of Islam *(bāb al ijtihad)*.

I am arriving at this conclusion without proclaiming, like others, that true Islam could *only* be found nowadays in Europe or the United States. The French Muslim Johan Cartigny once reduced this attitude to the pithy and provocative slogan: "True Islam is in exile."

This elitist view is voiced at times by American and European sufis who, at any rate, assume that only a choice few are privileged to attain pure Islam. One thing is, however, certain: Every born Muslim must be reconverted to Islam sometime during his life; Islam cannot be inherited.

In view of this, it is alarming when a level-headed and realistic man like Muhammad Asad toward the end of his long life revealed to me serious doubts as to whether, as in 1926, he would again find his way to Islam if he were a young man in today's Muslim world. With some bitterness he shared the frequently heard opinion that one could find lots of Muslims in the Orient, but precious little Islam these days, whereas the Occident had very few Muslims, but now much Islam.

With all this in mind I expect that Islam's revitalization and theological renewal, launched at the end of the 19th century and surfacing everywhere during the '70s will come to fruition in the 21st century, brought about by the combined force of European, American, and alert, courageous, and visionary Arab scholarship, primarily from Egypt, Pakistan and Malaysia. Many of these scholars have emigrated to the West—London, Washington, Los Angeles—and to Kuala Lumpur, because only there are they able to find the necessary working conditions, free of censorship and the threat to life and limb.

To arrive at a state of arrairs in which Islam can be perceived as an attractive, valid alternative to Western civilization in crisis requires a monumental effort of reform.

- The large legacy of the Hadith has to be screened once more, using modern historical and linguistic methods in order to ferret out possible falsifications of the chain of transmittors *(isnad)*.

- The immutable core of Qur'anic law *(shari'ah)* needs to be separated intellectually from the enormous edifice of Islamic jurisprudence *(fiqh)* which essentially is man-made and thus fallible.

135

- The hierarchical relationship between the Qur'an (primary source of Islam) and the Sunnah (secondary source) must be restated unequivocally.
- Those elements in Islamic tradition that are strictly a matter of *civilization* must be distinguished from their Islamic core, Islam as *religion*.

Facing these tasks is apt to make one's head spin![61]

At the same time, I had real problems with Borek's second debatable suggestion, which was to organize the *ethnic* German Muslims in a "Central Council of *German* Muslims," a specific interest group with its own publication. This would violate the fundamental Islamic principle to disregard any differences in skin color, language or nationality.

Any such organizational effort would be hampered by the indesputable fact that 97 percent of the Muslims in Germany are not Germans, a fact which has provided a welcome pretext for many a negative decision taken by German authorities. It is dangerous, of course, when potential xenophobia against non-European immigrants can be reenforced by being focused on a "foreign religion," Islam. But splitting the ummah in Germany into Germans and foreigners would truly be unfortunate and counterproductive. Could the 2.1 million Turks there really be expected to leave it to Germans to represent them as Muslims and, in the process, decide upon financial matters?

German Muslims will achieve the official recognition of Islam only shoulder to shoulder with their foreign brothers and sisters—or not at all. (The same applies to all Islamic communities in the West.)

---

61.   The following books give an idea of what is involved: Hussein Amin, *Le livre du musulman désemparé* (Paris 1992), based on the Arabic version of 1983; Taha Jabir al Alwani, *The Qur'an and the Sunnah: The Time-Space Factor* (Herndon, VA 1991); Muhammad Asad, *State and Government in Islam* (Gibraltar 1961), and *This Law of Ours* (Gibraltar 1987); Mohamed Karbal, "Western Scholarship and the Islamic Resurgence in the Arab World," *The American Journal of Islamic Social Sciences* vol. 10, no. 1 (Spring 1993); Imran Ahsan Khan Nyazee, *Theories of Islamic Law—The Methodology of Ijtihad* (Islamabad 1994); Abdul Hamid Abu Sulayman, *Towards an Islamic Theory of International Relations*, 2nd edition (Herndon, Va., 1993). My own contribution—*Islam 2000* (Cairo 1995; Beltsville, Md., 1996)—is so far available in Arabic and English only.

*

There is a sad story behind this discussion: the unfortunate split of Muslims in Germany. (This again is a situation typical for other European countries and the U.S.) It is natural for immigrants to organize by nationalities. Being a Muslim foreigner can be tough. Such associations along national lines are perpetuated by the support they receive from governments who want to monitor the emigration of dissidents. Unfortunately, these organization are again split along ethnic, political and religious lines. One is not merely a Turk, but—alas—Sunni or Alevite, Kurdish or Cherkess Turk, Sufi or orthodox—apart from the divisive question: Where do you stand with regard to Mustafa Kemal (or do you speak of Atatürk)? What was your opinion about the (now outlawed) Islamic Refah party and its "Islamic World View Organization" (IMGT) in Cologne? Such ethnic, political and religious diversity explains why Berlin as early as the mid 1980s was the seat of an umbrella organization comprising 27 (!) different Islamic groups and movements. This luxurious intra-Islamic pluralism explains why it is possible to find two Turkish mosques near each other in the same neighborhood: one (quite empty) run by the Turkish-Islamic Union (DITIB), a branch office of the agency for religious affairs in Ankara, and the other one (quite crowded) financed by guest workers, members of *Milli Görüş* (i.e., IMGT).

Largely responsible for this sorry organizational jumble is the fact that all the schisms plaguing the Islamic countries are mirrored throughout the world without a filter. The differences between Sunni and Shi'ite Islam, between mainstream believers and sufi orthodox brotherhoods and orthodox sects, heterodox brotherhoods and sects—each and every one of these differences plays itself out on American and European soil, not to mention political influences from Libya, Iran, Saudi Arabia and the Sudan.

Want to visit a Shi'ite mosque? No need to travel to Najaf, just take the road to the Außenalster district of Hamburg. Or would you care to compare sufi from the Sunni Naqshabandi brotherhood with those from the eclectic (pseudo Christian and pseudo Shi'ite) Bektaşi? No need to go all the way to Anatolia; Germany will do just fine. Would you like to interview Alawites, skillfully (but unsuccessfully) pretending to be Muslims? We'll do it on location, which again is Germany. Interested in observing representatives

137

of the Pakistani Ahmadiya sect, "excommunicated" by the Organization of the Islamic Conference? A stop over in Frankfurt suffices.

Muslims have been taught to view diversity as a blessing. But pluralism, too, can be exaggerated.

*

Even among the German Muslims organization leaves much to be desired. They all came across as if they had been trained for single combat, each on his own. As valuable as individual contributions may be, Islamic life depends on involvement in a Muslim community. One can be useful for Islam in Germany from a desk in Manama, as the ex-general secretary of the German Muslim League, or do so buried, as their curator, in the Islamic archives in Soest.[62] Being actively involved in the life of the Islamic community is a different matter.

One can certainly not begrudge the German Shi'ites for entertaining a center of their own in Hamburg and for issuing their own magazine.[63] And it is certainly legitimate for German sufi—Islamic mystics—to have their own center and their own publishing house,[64] although Islamic mysticism plays a far lesser role in Germany than in neighboring France. There, most of the major converts to Islam have been mystics following in the footsteps of the Andalusian *Shaykh al-akbar* (the Grand Master) Ibn al 'Arabi (born

---

62. A "Verein Zentralinstitut Islam-Archiv Deutschland" (Central Institute Islam Archive for Germany), a registered society, is located in Brüderstrasse 16, 59494 Soest, Germany, phone (02921) 14116. Here, too, the "Muslimische Revue" is published (manager: M.S. Abdullah).

63. The Islamic Center as well as the affiliated grand mosque are conducted by Dr. Ali Emari. Address: Schöne Aussicht 36, 22085 Hamburg, Tel. (040) 478041; They publish the periodical *Al-Fajr/Die Morgendämmerung* (phone 22 12 20).

64. One of them is the Tariqa Burhaniya Foundation in *Haus Schnede*, located in the Northern German town of Salzhausen, related to the Shadhiliya brotherhood. The periodical *Al-Sufi* is published in Dorfstr. 63, 03253 Trebbus, Tel. (035322) 31461. The publishers of *Turban Verlag* in the Black Forest town of Bonndorf, Salim and Hagar Spohr, are dedicated to the Naqshabandi brotherhood. See their publication of the teachings by the famous sufi master Nazim Adil al Haqqani from Cyprus, *Der Weg der Weggefährten*, Bonndorf 1991. Address: Schulstr. 15, 79848 Bonndorf, phone (07653) 962070. They also publish the magazine *Der Morgenstern*.

1165 in Murcia, d. 1240 in Damascus). He like the modern French mystics after him—Michel Chodkiewicz, Charles-André Gilis, as well as Eva de Vitray-Meyérovitch—moved, and still move in a dizzying speculative realm bordering on, and overlapping with, ancient gnosticism and pantheism.

Germany is different. Thanks to Turkish influence the sufi brotherhoods there are walking the traditional and sober path of an orthodoxy as promoted by the Naqshabandi dervishes, originally from Central Asia. No wonder that a German sufi woman, Michaela Mihriban Özelsel in Frankfurt is the most rational and scientifically oriented analyst of mystic experiences, after all, she is a professional psychologist.[65]

And yet: Does Germany, as currently (1998) really need 23 Muslim periodicals, among them, since 1924, the small format *Moslemische Revue*, the Muslim women's magazine *HUDA* in Bremen and the *Islamische Zeitung* in Weimar? Why not instead envisage *one* large, comprehensive transregional publication, e.g., through upgrading "Al Islam" (with "Al-Islam Aktuell") so far the liveliest, broadest, and most relevant journalistic product of Muslims in Germany, published by the Islamic Center in Munich.[66]

And what is the advantage in having many undercapitalized and technically outdated Muslim one-man publishers, such as the *Verlag Islamische Bibliothek* in Cologne,[67] or the *S.K.D. Bavaria-Verlag* in Munich?[68]—Why not have instead *one* major modern, highly efficient Muslim publisher?

It is an additional disadvantage of this maverick culture that it seems to breed deceptive advertisement. When somebody acts for the German Section of the (by now insignificant if not defunct) Islamic World Congress or the German Muslim League:[69] Does this not raise grand expectations? Both organizations were or are useful, but extremely small social circles with big names. To good to be true was also the still-born effort for the

65. See Michaela Özelsen, *Forty Days - The Diary of a Traditional Solitary Sufi Retreat* (Brattleboro, Vt., 1996), reviewed in *Igra* (San Jose), March 1997, p. 19.
66. *Al-Islam*, Wallnerstr. 1-5, 80939 Munich, phone (089) 325061/61.
67. *Verlag Islamische Bibliothek GmbH*, P.O.Box 83 01 35, 51034 Köln, Tel. (0221) 603111. Executive: M.A.Rassoul.
68. *SKD Bavaria Verlag*, P.O.Box 43 10 29, 80740 München, Tel. (089) 392088; Executive: Dr. A. Khafagy.
69. *Deutsche Muslim Liga e.V.*, P.O.Box 20 22 17, 20215 Hamburg. Secretary General: Abdulkarim Grimm. Abdullah Borek issues the League's very useful newsletter, the *DML Rundbrief*, from Manama.

establishment of an Islamic Party of Germany (IDP),[70] initiated by Mohy Eldin Louden in 1989 even though there were only about 50,000 Muslims eligible to vote as citizens. Not serious! Even in the federal State of North Rhine Westphalia, where the majority of German Muslim nationals live, such a political party would be useless, even at the local level. If the Muslims in Germany want to be recognized, they first have to be taken seriously; and if they want to be taken seriously, they first have to eliminate the faintest suspicion of fourflushing. For the foreseeable future, the political goals of German Muslims can only be pursued through the established parties, and through individual politicians sympathetic toward Islam, even if Muslims can never fully agree with any of their platforms.

Praise be to Allah that in Germany there are quite a few active German nationals, men and women, who are doing a solid job in working toward the understanding, recognition, and spread of Islam. Among them are Harun Behr, Muhammad Siddiq (Wolfgang Borgfeldt), Ahmad von Denffer, Bashir Dultz, Dr. Mehmet and Amina Erbakan, Abdul-Karim and Fatima Grimm, Hassan Haacke, Muhammed Herzog (a former priest) Muhammad Aman Herbert Hobohm, Abdul Hadi Hoffmann, Dr. Ayub and Asiye Köhler, Dr. Ibrahim Rüschoff, Yayha Schülzke, Ibrahim El-Zayat. And there are model institutions like the Haus des Islam (House of Islam)[71] in the Odenwald region south of Frankfurt with the associated Muslim boarding house Dar al-Salam (House of Peace), as well as numerous Islamic community centers across the entire Republic. So the many non-German activists are not alone.

Without high-pitched propaganda or street peddling, or busybody hysterics, dedicated people in these and other places—among them young bi-lingual and bi-national "third generation" Muslims—are steadfastly working for Allah's cause, with persistence and determination. Seminar upon seminar, youth camp after youth camp, one information week after the other, and from pilgrimage to pilgrimage—with unwavering faith, dedication and sincerity, in brotherhood—they perform the indispensable grass-roots work directed at individual hearts and minds. One has to patiently tend to the roots of the sapling rather than pluck the fruits before their time.

---

70. In 1989, an appeal to work on behalf of this *IDP* was published by Prof. Dr. Mohy Eldin Louden in the Munich magazine *Al-Islam*, no. 1, without success.
71. Haus des Islam, Schillerstr. 46, 64750 Lützelbach, Tel. (06151) 912019. Director: Muhammad Siddiq.

I am especially impressed by the systematic activities of the Muslim community in Munich, which is inspired by Ahmad von Denffer's charisma. It is no coincidence that since 1974 the first Islamic kindergarten and the first Muslim primary school (1981) are located in Munich. They were the first Islamic facility eligible for the employment of Muslim conscientious objectors (to the draft), to do their alternative civil service. The editors (since 1974) of the Al-Islam magazine are in Munich: so are the headquarters of both the Islamic Boy Scouts[72] and the relief organization *Muslime helfen e.V.* (Muslims Help).[73] Therefore, during the Rushdie affair it was quite natural for the Islamic community in southern Germany to assume the necessary authority to speak and be heard when condemning the Iranian-Shi'ite threats to kill the blasphemous writer without due process.[74]

Since 1976, the regular meetings of German Speaking Muslims (TDM) have become an institution and have taken a turn for the better, not just in organizational terms. The TDM owe a great deal to Muhammad Siddiq and Ahmad von Denffer. At first annual meetings, from 1981 on their number grew to three a year. The TDM have, however, become so crowded that several regional gatherings have recently been added to a main, again only annual event.

From the very beginning those meetings became instrumental for the solution of pressing problems: teaching Islam in schools; revision of history textbooks; umbrella organization for Muslims in Germany.[75]

---

72.   Founded and managed by Tilmann Schaible in 1988. Their motto: "Allahu akbar - Be Prepared". The lily in their crest is framed by a new moon and a five-pointed star.

73.   *Muslime helfen, e.V.*, is closely working with "Muslim Aid" (London). Among other things, the organization has been providing medical and food aid for Sudanese and Bosnian refugees. Address: P.O.Box 1607, 85740 Garching, Tel. (089) 32369500; account for donations: *Postgiroamt Frankfurt* no. 6569-604 (BLZ 500 100 60).

74.   At the time Ahmad von Denffer announced publicly that nobody was forced to carry out Khomeini's verdict. It was based on an error in legal interpretation, because apostasy (deserting from faith) must not necessarily be equated with high treason. In an open letter he wrote, "We do not approve of Iran's threat of assasination." See *Al-Islam* (Munich) no. 1 (1989): 9ff., 19.

75.   See Ahmad von Denffer (ed.), *Islam hier und heute, Beiträge vom 1.-12. Treffen deutschsprachiger Muslime (1976-1981)* (Cologne 1981), for summaries and decisions taken.

From 1980 until 1987, I gained a lot by participating in the winter meetings at the Bilal-Mosque in Aachen. These weekend meetings with book bazaar were not just instructive because of the lectures and workshops, but also because of the chance to meet new Muslims and engage in interesting table conversations.

These TDM are a stage for very colorful scenes, because the majority of participants are Muslims from abroad who take this opportunity to wear their national dress. Many a German Muslim as well unmistakably betrays "whether the spiritual midwives of his becoming a Muslim were Arabs, Turks or Pakistanis."[76] Even spies, from the German equivalent of the FBI, are apt to enjoy this lively picture of cultural diversity.

*

As in other countries, Muslims living in Germany frequently risk getting into conflict with their environment. In many respects a Muslim is living against the grain of the people around him and according to different values. Working at the assembly line, he is hardly ever given time for prayer. As a rule, canteens do not offer the choice of a proper Muslim diet. For home cooked meals it is difficult to find meat from animals slaughtered according to Islamic requirements.

It can be worse for the children. Girls are teased for wearing their headscarf. Their refusal to participate in mixed swimming classes or to wear a two piece bathing suit can be grounds for administrative sanctions. At least with regard to coeducational swimming classes, the Superior Administrative Court in Münster has fortunately decided in 1990 that the parents' rights can take precedence over the educational prerogatives of the State when they collide with religious convictions. In 1991, the same type of court in Bremen followed that precedence by excusing, too, a Turkish girl from mixed swimming classes for religious reasons. It was refreshing to hear from these courts that the interpretation in point of the Qur'an is essentially up to the parents, not to be challenged by governments or courts. Turkish parents thus can no longer be told by non-Muslims what the Qur'an "really" forbids or allows.

---

76. Ibid., p. 32.

High school history lessons are a major source of distress for Muslim children, especially when their textbooks contain passages which distort or denigrate Islam and its history. By way of reaction, the fifth annual TDM in 1977 decided to set up a schoolbook working group, The final result was a remarkable research project on Islam in the schoolbooks of the Federal Republic of Germany, with great idealism guided and promoted by Professor Abdoldjavad Falaturi, Director of the Cologne (now Hamburg) Islamic Scientific Academy, and by his non-Muslim collaborators, like Father Hans Vöcking and Udo Tworuschka.

They analyzed all of the 600 different titles approved for schools from 1979 to 1986 in the subjects of history, geography as well as Protestant and Catholic religion. The outcome was disconcerting and uncomfortably reminiscent of the problem of bureaucratic culpability *à la* Adolf Eichmann.[77] Can we rule out that violent attacks against Muslims—like the deadly 1993 arson attack on a Turkish family in Solingen, and the 1994 attack on the Islamic Center in Munich—are the final results of ugly representations of Islam in textbooks? With that in mind the late Professor Falutari published concrete textual suggestions for an objective treatment of Islam in schoolbooks, no matter where.[78]

Even if this became reality, it would not put an end to the second class status of 500,000 Muslim children in German schools, because religious classes teaching Islam can still not be taken for granted in German schools, even though Hans Krollmann, a former minister of culture for the federal State of Hesse, long admitted that equal treatment of Islam and Christian churches was strictly mandated by the German constitution. It was an obligation to "concede to religious and ideological pluralism what it demands."[79]

Some of the German federal States claim that such contingents were contingent on the previous official recognition of the Islamic community as a religious corporation. Others, like North-Rhine Westphalia are at least pre-

---

77. See *Studien zur Internationalen Schulbuchforschung* vol. 53. "Der Islam in den Schulbüchern der Bundesrepublik Deutschland" in Hans Vöcking et. al., *Analyse der katholischen Religionsbücher zum Thema Islam* (Braunschweig 1988).
78. Falutari, Abdoljavad, ed. *Der Islam im Unterricht. Beiträge zur interkulturellen Erziehung in Europa*, (Braunschweig 1991).
79. *Frankfurter Allgemeine Zeitung*, May 5, 1984.

pared to offer Islamic instruction in schools, but only along the lines of a government approved, objectionable curriculum. Other States again at least make classrooms available for Islamic instruction (the so-called Berlin-solution). Bavaria was the first State to allow and even support an Arab-German (de facto Muslim) private school. Berlin in 1995 licensed an Islamic primary school (Islamisches Kolleg Berlin, e.V.).

During Ramadan, workers and their kids can count on precious little sympathy. And on the first day of the Feast of Breaking the Fast (*'Id al Fitr)*, Muslim students are lucky to be excused from classes for that day.

A sadly amusing chapter is the one about how mosques get built (or not). In spite of the frequently shown solidarity of local parish priests and pastors, mosque building projects are mostly bogged down by all kinds of legal and not so legal maneuvers. Everybody can easily see for themselves the scenic similarities of the Bavarian foothills and the Bosnian landscape. But while a minaret is blending nicely into the Bosnian landscape, it evidently fails to do so in the Christian-occidental State of Bavaria. The aesthetic sensibilities of many a righteous city elder are obviously more partial to the ugly chimney of a factory building than to a graceful minaret.

Much too often building permits have to be fought over in court. In 1989, a Kehl citizen carried his crusade against the construction of a mosque all the way to the Federal Administrative Court, which he expected to protect him from the dreaded nightly disturbance by the call to morning prayer. Unfortunately for him, the mosque was going to be built in a neighborhood of noisy factories and of a church whose bells toll early.

Very revealing is the frequent haggling over the proposed height of a minaret. Zoning laws be damned, it must not be taller then the next church steeple! The fact that Muslims in Pforzheim succeeded in getting an 80-foot minaret built is a miracle of tolerance. Their brothers in Bobingen had their minaret sized down to 25 feet by the department of planning and development. Here again, the issue will ultimately be for a court to decide. In the city of Aachen, on the other hand, the Greens did not even bother to hide their purely political motives behind their delaying action against the expansion of a mosque that had become way too small.[80]

---

80. Islamisches Zentrum Aachen (Bilal Mosque), e.V., Professor-Pirlet-Str. 20, Tel. (0241) 820334. Principal officers: Dr. Salah ad-Din Nakdali and Dr. Mohammad Hawari.

About the the Green Party City Council Members' legally untenable objections to a new mosque, see *Die Zeit*, Oct. 12, 1990, no. 42.

Thus 20,000 Muslims from the area around Aachen had their constitutional right of practicing their religion severely curtailed. This is like declaring war against Islam itself.

But that is not enough. While most communities sooner or later will (or will have to) *issue* a building permit, they will not allow the *use* of the minaret as a minaret. There would be no legal objections if the same community at the same time would prohibit the churches from sounding their bells. This, however, they are reluctant to do. As if the principle of equal protection under the law did not apply. By arguing this particular point, Spanish Muslims have done better. Since 1994, *mu'adhdhin*s are allowed to call to prayer in this most Catholic country.

I sometimes ask myself the cynical question whether mosques would become more acceptable if the *mu'adhdhin* were sounding bells for prayers. Or if calling out loud is mandatory, should he perhaps drop his "Allahu akbar" in exchange for "ding dang dong?"[81]

It gives us pause to note how often Muslims have to sue for their rights in court. This may be one way of showing that the law will always prevail. But this is not the way to make a democracy work.

*

One would think that the problems of German Muslims come to an end with his passing away. Think again. Even a proper Muslim funeral meets resistance. A Muslim wants to be buried in a shroud, lying on his right side, facing Makkah. Very few cemeteries maintain sections accommodating these wishes. In addition to that, German cemetery regulations insist on the use of a coffin (and thus significantly prolonging the process of decomposition).[82]

But that is not yet the end. For Muslims, the rules of inheritance of the Qur'an obtain, where every conceivable line of inheritance is described in no lesser detail than by the German or French civil codes. And yet it

---

81. This idea was inspired by a Dutch cartoon.
82. If the deceased is both wrapped in a shroud and placed in a coffin, the time of decomposition lengthens from seven to ten years. See Ahmad al-Khalifa, "Das Begräbnis im Islam," *Al-Islam* (Munich) no. 3, 1989.

remains for a German probate court to process a German estate as directed in Book Five of the German Civil Code (BGB).

For Muslims living in Germany, the only way to hand down property in a manner consistent with Qur'anic laws governing inheritance is to make gifts while alive, or arrange everything as last will by testament. This remedy fails, however, if even so much as one potential Muslim heir won't play along.

*

One might assume that many of the above mentioned problems could be alleviated, if not altogether resolved, if government agencies and parliament had someone to turn to who really could speak for all Muslims in Germany, authoritatively.

The lack of such a spokesman has been discussed ever since the 2nd meeting of German-speaking Muslims on October 9 and 10, 1976 in Munich. The question was whether the cause of Islam is better served by support "from above" (model *Opus Dei*) or "from below"? My consistent response has always been that those are not mutually exclusive alternatives, but rather, two complementary options that should be pursued together.

"Support from above" means first and foremost engaging in efforts to gain governmental recognition for Islam. The idea is for Islam to have the same opportunities to thrive in public life that the Catholic, Lutheran and Reformed Churches, as well as the Jewish community, already enjoy. Such a recognition would quite obviously have far reaching consequences in many different areas—schools, income and church taxes, holiday regulations, protocol , access to the media, and much more.

From March 7 to 8, 1987, at the "House of Islam" in Lützelbach, I conducted a seminar about the conditions and prerequisites that would take us to our goal. This was based on a memorandum I had previously prepared on the establishment of a formal "Islamic Community" in Germany.

I explained to the audience that article 4 of the German constitution provided the basis for a recognition of Islam as a religious corporation under public law, thus guaranteeing the fundamental right to practice one's faith. How this is to be implemented derives essentially from still valid articles of the previous Weimar constitution of 1919. According to article 137 of the

Weimar Constitution, government agencies decide whether or not a religious community can be granted the status of a religious corporation (on the basis of its numerical strength, organization, democratic reliability, and promise of permanence).

While we agreed that there is a sufficient number of Muslims in Germany, they were not sufficiently organized. Thus, the foundation of an "Islamic Community in Germany" should have priority. We assumed, though, that even after becoming a duly incorporated entity, the Islamic community would be refused the presumption of "permanence" because most Muslims here are guest workers, with temporary residency permits only, in conformity with the fading dogma that "Germany is not an immigrant country."

The participants of the seminar thought that this dogma had already been rendered absurd by the normative force of facts to the contrary. Still, it will clearly take a long time before the Germans, in and out of government, come to realize that Islam has become the second largest religion in Germany as well as in England, France, and the United States, and that Islam is here to stay.

*

German Muslims, being neither pessimists nor fatalists, should set out to clear the hurdles for a future recognition of Islam by improving the organizational structure of Muslims in Germany.

What a publicly registered "Association of Muslims" would be able to achieve was enumerated in the following points which my son had listed as follows:

- Outside representation of all Muslims
- Election of a supreme imam in Germany
- Initiating the process for the official recognition of Islam
- Maintaining a central library, documentation center and archives
- Annual publication of an almanac (with prayer times, fasting schedules, holidays, addresses of mosques, schedule of events, bibliographies)
- Organizing meetings, exhibitions, hajj and other group tours
- Publishing a newsletter with classified ads, even for matchmaking between Muslim men and women

- Supporting the building of mosques.
- Offering of scholarships for needy Muslim students, especially in journalism and law.

Maybe one has to be a young man or woman to come up with such an idealistic project. But such dreams can be guideposts for a more concrete vision of the future. In fact, it was such strategic brainstorming that on December 12, 1988, led to the first nationwide cooperation of Muslims in the Federal Republic of Germany in the form of a "Permanent Workgroup of Islamic Communities in Germany."

This group seeded what was to become the *Zentralrat der Muslime in Deutschland—ZMD* (Central Council of Muslims in Germany), founded on November 27, 1994 in Cologne, with the Saudi-German physician Dr. Nadeem Elyas as president[83] and accompanied by some unexpected accolades.[84] In status and mission similar to the Central Council of Jews in Germany, ZMD's purpose is to function as a "contact group and a dialogue partner" for the federal government, governmental agencies, and other organizations. The claim rested on the fact that from its inauguration, ZMD was the leading Muslim organization in Germany, comprising and coordinating fifteen umbrella organizations with more than 1200 local Muslim communities and centers, representing about 70% of all the Muslims in the country.

Among the members of the ZMD are, e.g., the German Muslim League, the Muslim Student Association (*MSV*), and the Islamic Council in Germany (*Islamisches Konzil in Deutschland*). Yusuf Islam and Professor Annemarie Schimmel, e.g., serve on the ZMD's consultative board. The Milli Gürüsh organization (IMGT) does not participate, quite obviously because their primary interest is the re-islamization of Turkey.[85]

The ZMD in turn is a member of an Islamic umbrella organization at the European level—the Islamic Cooperation Council in Europe—whose secretariat is located in Strasbourg.

---

83. *Zentralrat der Muslime in Deutschland*, Vogelsänger Str. 290, 50825 Köln, tel./fax: (0221) 542616 or (02403) 24434.
84. As by Wolfgang Günther Lerch, in *Frankfurter Allgemeine Zeitung*, Dec. 1st., 1994.
85. According to official figures, every six hours a new privately financed mosque has recently been completed in Turkey. A large amount of money for that purpose flows in from Germany.

For the first time, the Central Council of Muslims in Germany impressively measured up to its own high expectations on June 28, 1995, when its president, himself a medical doctor, testified before the Health Committee of the German Parliament on the subject of brain death and organ transplantation. It is therefore not surprising that even the German President now receives the ZMD president as leading representative of Islam in Germany.

Whether or not the Central Council is to emerge as the *only* voice of Islam will largely depend on the ability of the Islamic community to smooth over existing theological idiosyncrasies among them. Remembering the restatements of Islamic doctrine as written by Al Ash'ari (d. 935) and Al Ghazali (d. 1111) will go a long way toward achieving a common denominator.[86] Formulating a theological consensus could also provide a helpful platform for the articulation of Islamic positions on topics like social market economy, the rights of women, and the Muslim approach to democracy and Human Rights.

For the time being, however, skepticism is in order. It will take a long time before the majority of Germans have warmed to the idea of Islam as an invigorating and colorful *German* phenomenon that one can live with—perhaps after realizing that wanting Islam and Muslims to just go away won't help.

But going on from there toward a full acceptance and inclusion of Islam, even that is a long road to hoe. Johann Wolfgang von Goethe pointed the way:

Tolerance should actually be but a passing attitude
that must lead to acceptance. To tolerate only is to insult.[87]

We are not there yet, of course. That is why Ahmad von Denffer was absolutely right when he observed a few years ago, "We are not taken seriously. What we enjoy in our subculture is the freedom of fools"[88]—only this, and nothing more.

I fear that even this limited tolerance has not grown lately, but rather dwindled in the wake of the Rushdie affair and the second Gulf War. These days, even Muslim loyalty to the constitution, their respect of human rights, and their democratic credentials are being openly questioned. This way,

---

86.   Both are printed in Arnold Hottinger, *Allah heute* (Zurich 1981).
87.   Goethe, *Maxime & Reflexionen,* Nr. 121.
88.   Ahmad von Denffer, *Islam hier und heute,* p. 69.

more and more obstacles are being piled up in order to frustrate any move toward a public recognition of Islam. The final chapter will elaborate on this problem.

BOGEYMAN ISLAM

Some changes affecting a new Muslim have been described in the previous pages. The novice Muslim is changing, but so is his environment and the way people look at and react to him. This is a dialectical, possibly even an escalating process which in individual cases can end in emigration.

The reaction of friends, family, neighbors and colleagues to the announcement "Thank God, I'm a Muslim!" depends on their general education, their level of sophistication, their heart, and above all, their own religious feelings. Indeed, some Protestant church districts in the Ruhr Valley demonstrated with their "Ecumenical 1996 holiday calendar for Jews, Christians and Muslims" how even competitive religious attitudes can have positive results.

My conversion to Islam did not cause me any problems, neither with family and friends, nor with colleagues at work. I was not treated like a "nut" in the throes of a mid-life crisis. To the contrary, after reading my first Islamic publications, "A Philosophical Approach to Islam" and "On the Role of Islamic Philosophy,"[89] a friendly correspondence ensued on the issue of Islamic *tawhid* as compared to the Christian concept of Trinity. However, only very few people had the presence of wishing me a happy Ramadan Festival (*'Id al Fiṭr*), or a blessed Feast of the Sacrifice (*'Id al Aḍha*) instead of a routine Merry Christmas.

Accepting my becoming a Muslim was especially difficult for my extremely Catholic mother, because she felt responsible (and thus liable) to God for this "misstep." In a letter I had tried—and failed—to build her a bridge by writing that "the Muslim sees Jesus as the most important prophet in a succession of Jewish prophets, because he could work miracles and was born of a virgin. The difference between the two religions can be very

---

89. Published by Verlag Islamische Bibliothek, Cologne, 1984.

big—or can be very small,—*as you wish.*" My mother was intent on seeing a *large* difference.[90]

I also did not experience any discrimination in my professional life. On February 6, 1984, three and a half years after my conversion, the German President Dr. Karl Carstens awarded me the Order of Merit of the Federal Republic of Germany. My "Diary of a German Muslim"[91] was distributed by the German Foreign Office to all German foreign missions in the Muslim world as an analytical tool. On February 13, 1986, Wolfgang Günther Lerch reviewed my "Diary" for the *Frankfurter Allgemeine Zeitung* under the title: "A German as Muslim—A Diplomat's Notes on His Religious Conversion." This did not make a lot of hay, neither did a multipage write-up with pictures of me and my wife in *Bild-am-Sonntag*, Germany's most widely circulated tabloid, on February 17, 1991. Until then, nobody had disputed the particular advantage for Germany to be represented by a Muslim in a Muslim country.

*

My relationship to representatives of the churches was also very pleasant. Many among them understood quite well that in an increasingly agnostic world, Christians and Muslims are sitting in the same boat. Instead of animosity, I sensed a kind of envious admiration of the powerful pull of Islam. On July 22, 1993, a senior representative of the Evangelical Church in Germany (EKD) declared in the Munich Mosque that he felt particularly at home with Muslims because they were talking about God in a straightforward and unaffected fashion which had unfortunately become rather rare in Protestant circles. This open, mutual understanding also distinguished a Christian-Muslim dialogue with my participation that took place from November 13–15, 1995 near Hannover between the EKD and the Royal-Jordanian Academy for the Study of Islamic Civilization (*Ahl al Bayt Foundation*).

---

90. About the problems of novice Muslims and their families, see Murad Hofmann, "How to tell mother?" *Al-Islam* (Munich) no. 5 (1985).
91. *Tagebuch eines deutschen Muslims*, Verlag Islamische Bibliothek, Cologne (1985), 1991, English version Cologne 1987.

But so far the chances for a successful dialogue have not yet extended to *theology*, but remain limited to an improvement of interpersonal relationships.[92] At the end of the Second Vatican Council in 1965, the Catholic Church had at long last let go off its claim to be the only road to redemption (*extra ecclesiam nullum salus*) and recognized Islam as one possible path to salvation. The efforts of the Tübingen theologian Hans Küng notwithstanding, Rome refused, however, to take the next logical and conclusive step to recognize Muhammad as leader on this path (and by extension the Qur'an as an authentic divine revelation).

At times, the Christian-Islamic dialogue has been fruitless, frustrating, even downright counterproductive. This was evident during one of Küng's lectures on November 19, 1988 in Algiers. After carefully presenting his view of Christianity and Islam, he was promptly asked, "If you believe what I just heard you say, then why are you still a Christian?" Küng had a ready rejoinder in his booklet "Pourquoi suis-je toujours chrétien?" ("Why am I still a Christian?"),[93] but the event had already veered onto the wrong track. Nothing is more deadly for the inter-religious dialogue than efforts at appropriating each other.

By and by, though, a rapprochement seems to be taking place also in the learned area of *theology*, as more and more Christian Bible scholars from both churches are beginning to return to the views of the earliest Christians—Jewish Christians and later Aryan Christians—about the nature of Jesus. Adolf von Harnack (d. 1930) had already pointed out earlier that the Apostles had never considered Jesus to be God, indicating that the so-called Apostolic Creed neither originated from the Apostles, nor reflects their convictions. The devastating indictment of the sources of the New Testament that resulted from new research since the 19th century added fuel to the fire. Particularly serious was the finding that the only Biblical passage touching on trinity in 1 John 5:7 is a forgery dating back no further than to the year 380.

---

92. Suggested reading for those interested in the full dimensions of the problem: Maurice Borrmans, *Wege zum christlich-islamischen Dialog;* Ismail Raji al Faruqi, *Trialogue of the Abrahamic Faiths,* 4th edition (Beltsville, Md., 1995); Michel Lelong, *Si Dieu l'avait voulu . . .* (Paris 1986); Murad Hofmann, "Zum Christlich-islamischen Dialog," *Al-Islam* (Munich) no. 4 (1986); Paul Schwarzenau, *Korankunde für Christen* (Stuttgart 1982).
93. The German version, *Woran man sich halten kann* (Paris, 1988) had been published earlier, in 1985 in Zurich.

Many Christian circles have developed mixed feelings about the unfortunate turn the 1st Ecumenical Council in Nicaea (325) took when a minority of bishops and prelates[94] had the audacity to decide that Jesus was "begotten" and not "created," and that he shared the nature of God Father (*homousio*, consubstantial). For these Christians, the most unfortunate part of this historical tragedy is the fact that this most crucial council in church history was called together and presided over by a pagan emperor, Constantine, who had suggested and pushed for the theological doctrine of consubstantiality to obtain *domestic political peace*.

To make a long story short, both Western churches, in contrast to the Orthodox churches, are currently engaged in efforts to return to "pre-Nicene" times. Thus, according to Rudolf Bultmann, Karl Rahner, Hans Küng, Paul Schwarzenau and John Hick Jesus is "just" a man "*uniquely chosen by God*," and according to Matthew Fox a mere "cosmic vision." The former corresponds to the Qur'an's Christology: "Christ, the son of Mary, was no more than a Messenger" (5:75).

The Protestant theologian Schwarzenau suggests that we are beginning to find ourselves in a "post-Christian age" containing "elements of a planetary religion." If this trend materializes, then the future will be free from any nonnegotiable theological obstacles on the path toward Christian-Islamic cooperation!

*

Following my conversion, I also did not experience any difficulties with *a-religious* people since they were usually honoring the thesis that religion is a private matter: a kind of tolerance founded on indifference. I had an amusing experience with this attitude before and during my first wedding on June 4, 1960, in the Harvard University chapel, which is now Unitarian. In the course of the mandatory marriage counseling session the minister merely wanted to ascertain that we were not hidden homosexuals. And high above the altar a caption read "Buddha, Confucius, Jesus, Moses, Muhammad"—in alphabetical order. Neutrality to the point of self-sacrifice. To each his own, what will it be?

In our thoroughly secularized world, I encountered a peculiar phenomenon: Some people shy away from presenting Muslims as Muslims, in order

---

94. Only five prelates were allowed to participate for Western Christianity with its decidedly Aryan convictions; the Pope was absent.

to quell from the outset any possible doubt about their intelligence. That happened to me frequently on my official trips as NATO's Director of Information, in the United States as well as in Europe. Whenever I was introduced, any mention of my being a Muslim was conveniently omitted or converted into an "interest in Islam."

On the other hand, it is clearly a sign of indolence or unforgivable negligence, when Islam's contribution to the Western cultural heritage is ignored outright. This is the case, for instance, in almost all general histories of philosophy published so far. *To know nothing about Islam is still not considered an educational deficit.*

*

Unfortunately, not all reactions to a Muslim conversion turn out to be harmless. What simmers in the European soul is a deep rooted irrational fear of Islam that has a long history and can easily lead to aggression. These anxieties are being nourished by long collective memories of ferocious battles waged between the Christian and Islamic world in the middle ages and before. Such a memory, lingering in the subconscious, is a constant reminder that Muslims ruled many centuries in Spain, Sicily, and Hungary. The crusades, too, contributed to Islamo-phobia. Their initial military achievements notwithstanding, the crusades triggered a culture shock among European knights when they had to realize that those despised "barbarian heathens" had brought forth a flourishing, sophisticated culture in the Near East that was superior to the Christian-European one in virtually all respects. Many a European became painfully aware, even then, of the symbolism that the Occident, i.e., the "western hemisphere of the setting sun," was only the evening that followed a morning which always rose in the Orient, the eastern "hemisphere of the rising sun."

Add to that, the worries about the revitalization of Islam that has manifested itself over the past decades, the more worrisome since it directly contradicts the prognostications of all expert analysts in Oriental Studies. When Max Henning's German Qur'an translation was first published in 1901,[95] the author in his preface wrote that Islam's "political role had obviously run its course." Considering the almost blanket colonization of the

95. Possibly a pseudonym for August Müller (Professor of Oriental Studies in Königsberg).

Islamic world at that time, his prognosis seemed to be a safe bet. For the first fifty years of this century, Islamologists were so convinced of the impending demise of their subject that much like botanists and anthropologists, they rushed head on into analyzing and describing Islam and its people exhaustively before both were to vanish. It was taken for granted that such a primitive aboriginal religion and its superstitious, obscurantist followers would whither in the sun of Western modernity.

It was therefore even more shocking, even provocative, to witness how developments since could climax in a Shi'ite State, Iran, which has been standing up to the United States since 1979, and Afghan *mujahiddin* forcing the demoralized army of a superpower out of their country.

Islam's obstinate refusal to exit the world stage is seen by many in the West as an almost insulting anachronism, especially with the triumph of the "capitalist" system over Communism. Since then, people in the Islamic world have noted with growing discomfort symptoms of a neo-imperialist cultural triumphalism in the West. This attitude found its classical manifesto in the book "The End of History"[96] by Francis Fukuyama, erstwhile head of the State Department's Office of Strategy and Planning, as well as in Bernard Lewis and Samuel P. Huntington's thesis about the impending clash of civilizations, mainly between the West and the East.[97] These fundamentalist beliefs of modernity, which are widely espoused in Postmodernist circles as well, hold that Western civilization (meaning the American Way of Life) is, in the terminology of Gottfried Leibnitz (d. 1716), "the best of all possible worlds." It is therefore considered to be *the* value system destined to *dominate* the history of mankind for now and forever. The values of the Occident, *its* political and economic system, *its* international laws, *its* technology and the hypotheses of *its* natural sciences serve as the *obligatory model* for the rest of the world. The only options left to non-Western mankind are either total surrender to the process of globalization (Muslims like to call this "MacDonalidization" or "Cocacolization"), or to become marginalized into insignificance without a home page on the INTERNET.

---

96. Francis Fukuyama, *The End of History and the Last Man* (New York 1993). The article appeared in 1991.
97. Samuel P. Huntington, "The Clash of Civilizations," *Foreign Affairs* vol. 72, no.2 (Summer 1993). This was preceded by the article "The Roots of Muslim Rage" by Bernard Lewis (*The Atlantic* vol. 266, no. 3 [September 1990]) which already discussed the conflict between the two cultures in question.

The abovementioned authors agree that in addition to the Confucian civilization, only one other is resisting this globalization and deterritorializa-
tion of Western culture: Islam. It seems indeed to be the only one hazard-
ing an *alternative* to Western civilization at its consumerist peak.[98]

This is why Lewis and Huntington are predicting a collision between
these two cultures. And this is why the then NATO Secretary General,
Claess, had called upon the military planners of the Alliance to prepare for
a military North-South conflict. The Viennese trauma "The Turks are coming!"—is making a come back . Once again, Islam provides the enemy.

Apart from that (but equally significant), Western mentality is shaped by
the uninhibited demonization of Muhammad from the Middle Ages up to
this very day. His defamation in Europe as a cunning fraud, an epileptic,
lecher, even a hellhound—Rushdie still calls him *Mahound*—is not just a
thing of the past. Annemarie Schimmel observed in that context: "More
than any other figure in history, Muhammad aroused fear, hatred, even con-
tempt in the Christian world, and when Dante banishes him into the deep-
est pits of hell in his *Divine Comedy,* he simply expresses the feelings of
countless Christians."[99] Indeed, in spite of the blasphemy statute in our
criminal code, the Prophet of Islam, revered by more than a billion people
around the world, is still treated like an outlaw in Germany and the rest of
Europe, and slandering him is very politically correct.

*

As a Muslim, one senses these manifold and deeply rooted resentments
of Islam day in, day out—at least in the form of a "double standard."

It is really quite remarkable to see how willingly the West tolerates a
teeming religious supermarket where (just about) anybody can hawk their
wares: Rudolf Steiner's anthroposophists, Buddhists, Hare Krishna apostles, followers of Indian shamans like Carlos Castaneda, worshippers of

---

98.　In direct response to Fukuyama (*The End of History and the Last Man*) I had
called my second book *Der Islam als Alternative*: Diederichs: Munich 1992; 3rd
edition 1995; English translation: *Islam: The Alternative*, Reading (U.K.): Garnet,
1992; second enlarged edition by amana publications, Beltsville (U.S.) 1997.
99.　Annemarie Schimmel, *Und Muhammad ist Sein Prophet*, 3rd. edition
(Munich 1995), p. 7.

female goddesses like Christa Mulack[100] and adepts of ghastly satanic cults. Movie star Richard Gere's embrace of Buddhism does not provoke any negative reactions. There's only *one thing* that you'd better stay away from to avoid trouble: Becoming a Muslim.

Time and again the media features reports about orthodox Judaism, primarily about the Lubavichers in Jerusalem and New York, and they talk with due respect and emphasis about the separation of the sexes, arranged marriages, religious hairstyles, clothes and head covers, dietary rules, ritual slaughter, and the rejection of pork. What never comes up is any suggestion that Jewish women's rights might be violated, or that those customs could ever be primitive, if not manifestly fanatic. But these are precisely the labels affixed to Muslims whenever their practices are described.

These double standards become most conspicuous whenever the media reports on terrorism. In the past nobody would refer to the "Catholic Hitler," and rightly so, or talk about "Stalin, the Orthodox Christian." Nowadays one properly avoids any emphasis of the Serbian leader Karadic, as a "Christian." The moment an Arab takes up a weapon, however, he is branded as "Muslim"—even if he is a Palestinian Christian or a godless Baathist (i.e., Fascist).

It did not occur to anybody to call the nuclear bombs dropped on Hiroshima and Nagasaki "Christian." However, when a Muslim country is suspected of building a nuclear device, everybody starts talking about a "Islamic Bomb."

I also have a sensitive ear for the reservation of the adjective "fanatic" for Muslims. Qadhdhafi and Saddam Hussein are fanatics, Milosovic is not. Assassinations in Catalonia, the Basque region, or Northern Ireland are not perpetrated by "fanatic Basques," or "fanatic Catholics," but by "members of the ETA" or "radical elements of the IRA." This development has gone to such absurd lengths that a Muslim can already be dismissed as a fanatic if he is caught doing no more than praying, fasting, and staying away from booze. If he wears sideburns, he is identified as an obscurantist with violent tendencies and runs into difficulties getting through customs. (The same beard on Ché Guevara was of course considered progressive.)

---

100. *Auf den Spuren der Göttin*, (Marl 1992).

Journey to Makkah

*

An even more serious development over the last fifteen years has been the degree of caricature, even outright distortion of Islam in several media, and the systematic fanning of fear of Islam and its followers. German Muslims were particularly affected by books penned by Peter Scholl-Latour, Gerhard Konzelmann (*Die islamische Herausforderung* [Islam's Challenge], 1981), Bassam Tibi and Rolf Stolz (*Mullahs am Rhein* [Mullah's at the Rhine], Munich 1994; and *Kommt der Islam?* [Islam—is it coming?], Munich 1997). German Muslims remember with horror recent incendiary TV broadcasts like "Terror in Allah's Name" (ARD, Bayern 3, on September 15, 1994).[101] This paved the way for BUNTE magazine to ask on January 19, 1995, whether "the center of our threat had not shifted from Moscow to Makkah?" They were probably safe to assume that by then hardly any reader would deny that.

Hardly anybody jeopardizes religious peace in Germany more than Bassam Tibi, a Syrian political scientist teaching in Göttingen, a former Marxist and currently what might be called a "cultural Muslim." If I read him correctly, he is endlessly fascinated by the "Project of Modernity," a child of the European Enlightenment. Ignoring how much the rationality of man has been discredited, especially in the 20th century and in the Occident, he presents Islam as a crass antithesis to the "Age of Reason," as an irrational and fundamentally totalitarian religion unable to contemplate peace.[102] Typical for that was a SPIEGEL article of his in 1994 bearing a titillating headline *"Wie Feuer und Wasser"* (Like Fire and Water) and a misleading quotation from the Qur'an. In this article he argued again that

---

101. Muhammad Aman Herbert Hobohm provided an excellent analysis of the anti-Islamic prejudice in the German media: *Islam and Muslims as Perceived by Government and Media in Germany* (Contribution to the annual convention of the Royal Jordanian Academy in Amman).

102. His most widely read publications are probably: *Die Krise des modernen Islams* (Frankfurt 1991); *Die Verschwörung, Das Trauma der Arabischen Politik* (Hamburg 1993); *Islamischer Fundamentalismus, moderne Wissenschaft und Technologie* (Frankfurt 1992); *Der Islam und die Probleme der kulturwellen Bewältigung sozialen Wandels* (Frankfurt 1985); *Im Schatten Allahs - Der Islam und die Menschenrechte* (Frankfurt 1994). In his writings he maintains, among other things, that "the Arab Orient would have stayed underdeveloped even if it had not been colonized." This says more about the author himself than about the Orient.

"Islam and human rights are mutually exclusive," because Islamic law segregates "Muslims from those civilizations which support human rights."[103] Tibi advises Muslims living in Europe to develop an "Euro-Islam" which is unreservedly in line with the principles of "modernity"—with lots of Europe and very little Islam.

German Muslims gratefully acknowledge the fact that the excesses described above have begun even to rankle non-Muslims. In 1992, Gernot Rotter managed to discredit Konzelmann more than hardly any other author before him, destroyed through literary critique.[104] In 1993, Verena Klemm and Karin Hörner[105] did the same to Scholl-Latour, and in the same year Dorothea Bölke[106] debunked Scholl-Latour, Konzelmann, and Bassam Tibi. In a similarly devastating dispute with Tibis' beliefs, Goltschehre Jung and Marfa Heimbach pointed out in 1994 that while Tibi is continuously warning of the "Islamic-fundamentalist challenge" to Europe, he often condemns as fundamentalists those who even as much as "use the words 'Qur'an' or 'Islamic'." Those two Tibi critics arrive at the same conclusion, namely, that the "massive one-sidedness of his depiction" is bound to foster an atmosphere with the very potential for hate, which led to the Holocaust 50 years ago, and currently to the mass murder of Muslims in former Yugoslavia."[107]

Other instances of post-modern cultural racism are the theses advanced by Mark Heller, who states that within in a collective global movement toward democracy and human rights the Muslim world constitutes a negative exception[108]—as if Muslims were congenitally incapable of democra-

---

103. Bassam Tibi, "Wie Feuer und Wasser," *Der Spiegel* no. 37 (1994): 170–172.
104. Gernot Rotter, *Allahs Plagiator. Die publizistischen Raubzüge des "Nahostexperten" Gerhard Konzelmann* (Heidelberg 1992).
105. Verena Klemm and Karin Hörner, *Das Schwert des Experten - Peter Scholl-Latours verzerrtes Araber- und Islam-Bild* (Heidelberg 1993).
106. Dorothea Bölke, "Drei Mann in einem Boot: Der islamische Fundamentalismus bei Peter Scholl-Latour, Gerhard Konzelmann und Bassam Tibi," in *Das Schwert des Experten.*
107. G. Jung and M. Heimbach, "Bassam Tibi - Ansichten über europäische Moderne und islamischen Fundamentalismus," *Religionen im Gespräch. Interreligiöser Dialog zwischen Tradition und Moderne* (Balve) no. 3 (September 1990).
108. Mark Heller, "The Middle East: Out of Step with History," *Foreign Affairs* vol. 59, no. 1: 155ff., 188–199.

cy. The German Islam scholar Gudrun Krämer (Berlin) was instrumental in impressively refuting this thesis in an essay-collection under the title "Democracy without Democrats?"[109] Almost all of these studies arrived at the conclusion that in the Muslim world there is no substantial link between religion and despotism, and that being a Muslim does not exclude being a democrat. On the other hand, it was noted that undemocratic regimes in the Muslim world are not under any Western pressure to democratize, only under pressure exerted by *Islamic* reform movements. In other words: According to those orientalist authors, the only danger Islam currently poses is for third world despots, but not for Europe.

*

Those who wish to single Muslims out as structural enemies of democratic constitution are misjudging the comprehensive Islamic human rights system anchored in divine legal prescriptions,[110] its proven democratic potential, and its democratic entelechy; they are also overlooking the vast Islamic protection of the rights of religious minorities (*siyar*). For centuries, Muslim legal scholars have also been developing the status and the legal responsibilities of Muslims living abroad in non-Muslim countries. Above all, it was the great al Mawardi (d. 1058), eminent scholar of Islamic public and constitutional law, who argued that in principle these Muslims *have to abide by the laws of their host country*.

The Hanafite school of law even taught that Muslims living in a Christian region are entitled to collect interest on capital since the Qur'anic laws governing financing and commerce did not apply there.[111] Given this kind of long legal tradition, how can anyone summarily accuse German Muslims of being born enemies of a democratic constitution?

People who take it upon themselves to comb through the Qur'an for intrinsic human rights shortcomings should proceed in kind with the New

---

109. Ghassan Salamé (ed.), *Democracy without Democrats?—The Renewal of Politics in the Muslim World* (London/New York 1994). See also my review in *The Muslim World Book Review* (Leicester) vol. 16, no. 1 (1995): 36–39.

110. See the chapters "Human Rights" and "Republic or Monarchy?" in Murad Hofmann, *Islam: The Alternative*, footnote 10, pp. 111 ff. and 69 ff.

111. Khaled Abou El Fadl, "Islamic Law and Muslim Minorities," *Islamic Law and Society*, vol 1, no. 2 (1995).

Testament. They would find there, for example, extremely questionable passages as in Paul's 1 Corinthians: "It is good for a man not to touch a woman" (7:1), or "The wife has not power over her own body, but the husband . . ." (7:4), or "Are you without a wife? Do not seek a wife" (7:27). Even more disturbing are his remarks in his first epistle to Timothy: "Let the woman learn in silence with all subjection. But I suffer not a woman to teach, nor to usurp authority over the man, but to be in silence. For Adam was first formed, then Eve" (2:11 ff.). In addition, one could gleefully recite 1 Peter: "Likewise, you wives, be in subjection to your husbands" (3:1).

Efforts such as these aimed toward "proving" the incompatibility of Christianity with the United Nations Charta of Human Rights would simply be stupid, misleading, and therefore dangerous. Why is this very method used to move against Islam?

*

Small wonder then that the above mentioned cultivation of anti-Islamic sentiments should leave its mark in international politics. Haiti and Algeria are striking examples for that. In both countries, fundamentalist leaders came to power in democratic elections; in both countries, the democratic franchise was thwarted by military coups. In the first case, the United Nations took action, assisted by U.S. Marines; in the latter case, government offices all over Europe heaved a sigh of relief, since the fundamentalist in question was not the Christian Aristide, but the Muslim Abbasi Madani.

From a Muslim perspective, double standards were also applied to the conflict in Bosnia. Here, as was the case with Kuwait, a small member state of the United Nations was occupied by a neighboring country. But the United Nations only took decisive and effective action only where oil interests were at stake. In Bosnia, the victims were "Muslims," but their tormentors were never identified as orthodox Serbian Christians (or Catholic Croat Christians), although the crazed Serbian thirst for revenge for a battle dating back 600 years (on the Kosova Polje—the blackbird field) has been, and is, kept alive by the Greek-Orthodox and Serbian-Orthodox patriarchy. The repeated assertions that Western inertia in the face of massacres and "ethnic cleansing" in Bosnia-Herzegovina were not motivated by religion, but rather by more banal, selfish and interest-driven reasons of national politics, are mostly true. Yet all of the Muslims believe that a degree of *subconscious* religious prejudice did affect the Bosnia conflict. The West failed in a similar fashion when Constantinople was lost to the Turkish Sultan Mehmet II in 1453. Stephen Runciman offers an instructive account of how the hatred which the Catholics in Paris, Rome, and Venice felt for the renegade, heretic Eastern Church caused the Eastern Roman Empire to be abandoned to the Turks.[112] For the Islamic world it remains inconceivable that the West would not have interfered right away if things had been reversed: if the Serbs had been Muslims, but committing the same crimes, and the Bosnians had been Christians, but suffering the same fate. We are all convinced that if this had happened, the West would have rallied in the name of human rights, the United Nations Charter, and Western humanism and immediately taken military action against those Muslim barbarians. The way I see it, neither would there have been an arms embargo against a helpless Catholic Bosnia.

Managing the crisis on the Balkans, the West flouted all principles and lessons that are drilled year after year on NATO's crisis management exercises like HILEX and WINTEX. For Muslims, this leaves but *one* conclusion: Indifference to an Islamic people in Europe. This is certainly not fair to many politicians and soldiers who had decided in principle not to get involved for reasons of neutrality and noninterference in foreign affairs. Honor also to the American senator who exclaimed, with Greenpeace in mind, "If only the Bosnians were dolphins!" All of this, including the involvement of NATO which came at last (and much too late) in the Fall of 1995, does not change the fact that millions of Muslims, primarily in third world countries, will speak now and for a long time to come with cynicism and bitterness of the Western ideals of human rights and democracy. Already, I frequently hear young Arabs ask sardonically whether human rights were perhaps blond and blue-eyed.

*

Muslims in Germany could be accused of being overly sensitive in spotting anti-Islamic bias. In light of numerous physical attacks on (mostly

---

112. Steven Runciman, *The Fall of Constantinople 1453* (Cambridge 1964).

Muslim) foreigners, however, one has to admit that their preoccupation is understandable, especially given Germany's history of National Socialist chauvinism. Only half a century has gone by since my fatherland was engaged in killing large numbers of German citizens simply for being *different* in religion, clothing, traditions, or for speaking with an eastern European dialect. The horrendous Holocaust was made possible because a pervasive anti-Semitism which stifled any moral scruples by the sheer force of perverted and purely subjective *ethical convictions*. The great worry among Muslims in Germany is that a similar mechanism can be set in motion which this time around would turn against another *Semitic* tribe: the Arabs and their religion, a nontaboo form of anti-Semitism which would target even ethnic German Muslims as "Arabs by choice." (Even my mother said, "Let him stay with *his* Arabs!" when she received my last postcard from Makkah shortly before her death.)

We are being reassured that nobody wants to see this happen. I would like to believe that. But if that is the case, those remote bureaucratic masterminds of mischief, potential perpetrators with pen and paper who hide behind their desks, will have to stop playing with fire and incendiary assertions about Muslims being enemies of the constitution who do not respect human rights and are intent on establishing a theocratic Mullah regime in an "Islamic Republic of Germanistan." With the critical background I described in mind one can only hope that in the future criticism of Islam will be handled with more care in Germany, and some media people will do so. At the same time, however, Muslims and their friends are beginning to encounter another disturbing phenomenon: Positive sentiments, even sympathies toward Islam are becoming *politically incorrect*.

As early as in his *"La démocratie en Amérique"* (Democracy in America), Charles Alexis de Tocqeville (1805–1859) had pointed out that even liberal democracies harbor totalitarian mechanisms controlling public opinion. And so democratic and liberal America had its witchhunts, the next to last one when Senator Joseph McCarthy (1905-1957) hunted down *"un-American* activities." McCarthyism is not dead, although in today's USA the study of socialist ideas is not considered subversive anymore. Today, the opponent is accused of *politically incorrect* thinking, which amounts to much the same phenomenon in new terminological dress. People in the Unites States open themselves up to this accusation—which is the political and academic kiss of death—whenever they raise the faintest suspicion of questioning one of three taboos: the equality of men and women, the equality of Black and White, and the unconditional linkage of American foreign policy to that of Israel.

In the Winter of 1994 a conference took place in Vienna on "The Europe of Religions Between Religious Wars and Civil Tolerance," where Robert Spaemann made the undisputed statement that in the name of liberal universalism, an illiberal climate was spreading in today's Europe, because antidogmatism was proving to be at least as zealous as dogmatism itself. According to him, antidogmatic relativism is the last manifestation of European universalism. In short, a liberalism which places the liberal system at the core of a secular pseudo-religion is as intolerant an ideology as any other system of thought.[113]

This is indeed the background for the force-feeding of "politically correct" opinions in Germany and elsewhere. There are, however, differences in the kind of taboos to be observed: In the United States a positive attitude to Islam is not (yet) incorrect, in Germany—and in England—on the other hand, it is. (My British publisher in Reading told me on a visit on October 2, 1995, that English bookstores had begun to shy away from displaying my book in their store windows. It was not safe anymore openly to display pro-Islamic literature.)

I became an early victim of exactly those in the media world who act as self-appointed guardians of civic virtues. In the beginning of 1992 when the Eugen Diederichs Publishing House announced "Islam: The Alternative" for the end of March, the mere title of the book caused ARD television and BILD-am-Sonntag (the largest national German TV network and the most popular German daily tabloid) to launch a journalistic broadside against me. I was accused of advocating polygamy, the beating of women, chopping off hands, and the stoning of adulterers (*BILD*, 22 March 1992). They even claimed that I forced the female staff in my embassy in Rabat to wear head scarves (*BILD*, 29 March), and that I had already driven one of my coworkers to suicide (*BILD*, 5 April). All of this came to a head in the first of these three articles which carried the following statements made by a vice-president and legal expert (!) of the German Social Democratic Party (SPD), "This man is intolerable as ambassador. Foreign Minister Genscher should quickly read this book and make sure that a man like this will no

---

113. Quoted in *Frankfurter Allgemeine Zeitung*, 7 December 1994, p. N5.

longer represent our country." (At that time, banning people from the civil service for political reasons had not yet been the leftist thing to do.) For her (the above mentioned vice president of the SPD), my book was "the product of a pretty naive macho who does not even know our constitution . . ."

Ms. Däubler-Gmelin had to admit later that she had not even read the incriminated book when she called upon the Foreign Minister to read and act upon it. How could she? At that time, it had not even been in print.

When the media finally investigated me—*after the fact*—and proceeded to read my book—*after the fact*—they found that the book did not support the allegations leveled against me.[114] The Qur'an was right again: "And guesswork is no substitute for truth" (53:28).

During those weeks—the weeks of Ramaḍan—I kept on fasting with equanimity, but I had to think more often of the Qur'anic verse which says:

> Do men think that they will be left alone on saying, We believe, and that they will not be tested? (29:2)

But I was also mindful of "And Allah is sufficient as defender" (4:132). My passivity in the face of an increasingly intense media campaign against my person left many of my colleagues puzzled. And yet I was—and I still am to this day—convinced that the truth of all these invectives was not the issue at all. These attacks were aimed beyond my person, and directed at Islam in general, and in particular at Muslims in Germany. I was guilty all right: My positive attitude to Islam had been *politically correct* up to 1990—but not anymore in 1992. This is the only explanation of how representatives of the media as well as politicians could so readily dismiss the cardinal rule of their profession—*audiatur et altera pars*. There was no need to hear my side of the story—I had already confessed to the most important point: being a Muslim.

In the meantime—in the Fall of 1995—there was a second attempt of media-induced *political correctness* in an Islamic context. This time it hit a much more prominent figure, the doyenne of Islamic studies in Germany, Annemarie Schimmel, formerly of Harvard University. The *Börsenverein*,

---

114. *DER SPIEGEL* wrote on March 30, 1992: "In reality the jurist with a Ph.D. from Harvard expressly advocates monogamy and rejects violence in marriage." In *DIE ZEIT*, Fredy Gsteiger wrote on May 15, 1992: "The authors of those salacious stories about the purposed excesses of an Ayatollah under the black-red-gold banner [Germany's colors] obviously failed to read Hofmann's two hundred pages."

the German Book Traders' Association, had the temerity to award their annual Peace Prize to her, a scholar sympathetic to Islam and its mysticism, and a specialist on Jalal al Din Rumi and Muhamad Iqbal, who is highly regarded in the Islamic world, particularly in Pakistan. When asked in that context about the Rushdieaffair, Ms. Schimmel condemned Khomeini's death-*fatwa* as "heinous" and "appalling," a legal opinion which was politically correct, but at the same time she stated that Rushdie had "hurt the feelings of a large number of believers in a very nasty way." She said she had "actually seen Muslims in tears because of this book." Even as "a non-Muslim and religious historian" she declared herself shocked, even though it is only a novel." This statement of fact and her emotional involvement were politically *incorrect*!

Gernot Rotter, her former student and colleague who interviewed her for *SPIEGEL* magazine, summarily rejected the depictions of the impact the "Satanic Verses" had on the Islamic world, "I won't budge: Muhammad is not really denigrated by Rushdie."[115]

As a result, a campaign was launched by the German Pen Club and the media which was to go on for months until the award ceremony on October 15, 1995. The general tenor was that Professor Schimmel was unfit to receive the prize because she was studying her field, Islam, with a highly inappropriate degree of affection. The controversy surrounding the Peace Prize seemed to consume the entire Federal Republic up to the very day of the award. Appropriately so, considering the dire consequences for the freedom of thought and opinion in Germany, the German Book Traders' Association had successfully been pressured into withdrawing the award. Thus the chair of Oriental Studies in Bonn, Stefan Wild, gave a radio interview as late as October 14, pointing out that the media were quite obviously engaged in the ancient ritual of punishing Ms Schimmel as the bearer of bad news—or in this case unwelcome messages. This was a mild censure among colleagues; Professor Wild could have just as easily upbraided Gernot Rotter for his eurocentric arrogance.

When President Roman Herzog agreed to award the prize in person on October 15, 1995, at the Frankfurt Paulskirche, he was perfectly aware of the stakes for the cultural and political climate in Germany. And it was for that good reason that both, the lord mayor of Frankfurt, Petra Roth, and Roman Herzog spoke of the "enemy image Islam" in German heads. The

---

115. *DER SPIEGEL*, May 21 & 22, 1995, pp. 214–216.

Federal President in his *laudatio* took express exception to the practice of media imposing *"political correctness,"* a development which might violate basic civic and constitutional rights, without recourse. Yes, indeed: What *is* to become of us if people can be silenced and gagged simply for reporting facts which for ideological reasons are not supposed to exist? What indeed, if German professors are allowed to take it upon themselves to decree to a billion other (unloved) people what to think and feel—and what not? God save Germany and the world—not only the Muslims—from the intolerance of "liberal" fundamentalists—and their obsession with the Muslim bogeyman.

Afterword

Although this book does not appear to follow any preconceived order, it is still organized around the five pillars of Islam, which are the profession of faith ("A Philosophical Approach to Islam), prayer (Five Times a Day, as Directed), paying taxes ("Money Dearest"), fasting ("On the Proving Ground"), and the pilgrimage ("Journey to Makkah").

In addition, it deals with other important commandments that define Islamic religious practice: The prohibition of addictive drugs ("Soberingly Sober"), the prohibition of pork ("At the Table with Muslims"), Islamic ritual slaughter ("At the Table with Muslims"), belief in predestination ("Fatalists with a Purpose"), animal sacrifice ("Money Dearest"), marriage ("Cherchez la Muslimah"), the propagation of the faith ("Islam in Germany ... A German Islam"), and the willingness to make sacrifices for one's faith (*jihad*) in the final chapter.

Therefore, in spite of its autobiographical frame, this book is intended first and foremost as a practical guide—for the road *toward* Islam, and for the road *of* Islam; the Muslims call it *sabil Allah*—the Path of God.

M. W. H.

INDEX

—A—

abortion, 111
Abraham, 12, 14, 17
accident(s), 22, 60
adhān, 19
adoption, 113
agnosticism, 38
Albrecht, 34
alcoholics, 57
Algiers
   war in, 29
appetizers, 75
Arabi Ibn al, 51, 138, 112
Arabic, 50
'Arafah, 21
Aristide, 162
Asad, Muhammad, 28, 106, 131, 132, 135
Aschaffenburg, 80
Ash'ari al 149
Atatürk. *See* Kemal
Azmani, 22, 25
Azwer, 9

—B—

bakshish, 8, 118, 122, 124, 125
Balanchine, 35
Baqī al, 6
basmala, 70
Behr, Harun, 140
Bejart, Maurice, 131
Benjedid, 48
Bhutto, 107
Bilal Mosque, 141
birth control, 110

Nöldecke, 129

—O—

O.A.S., 30
Omar, 5
original sin, 39
Osman, 106

—P—

Paret, 129
paternalism, 104
Paul, 38, 40
Pawlowa, 35, 113
Peters, 83
Philos, 39
Plotinus, 39
Pohle, 82
polygamy, 103
pork, 55
prayer
    texts, 49, 50
prayer niche, 5, 47
prayer rug, 53
preacher, 48
predestination, 79

—Q—

Qiblatain, 6
Qubā', 6
Qur'an, 14, 25, 32
    translation, 33

—R—

rajm, 23
Rahner, 154
rak'ah, 45
Ramadan, 31
Rassoul, 27
riba, 93
Rilke, 36
Rocher, 131
Rosenberg, 82

Rotter, 160
Rüschoff, 140

—S—

sa'ī, 14
Sachnowsky, 34
Saddam Hussein, 88
Sadr ud-Din, 128
Safā al, 14, 24
Salibi, 14
Sarah, 14
Schimmel, Annemarie, 51, 148, 156, 166, 167
Schmidt, 84
Scholl-Latour, 159, 160
Schülzke, 140
Schuon, 51
Schwarzenau, Paul, 154
Schweigger, 129
Shabassy el, 132
shari'ah, 135
Shawn, 35
Siddiq, 140, 141
Sidi Muhammad, 75
silver utensils, 64
Simon, 47
slaughter, 19
solidarity, 65, 120
Spaemann, 165
spells, 87
Steiner, 157
Stevens, 131
stoning, 19
stress, 52
Sunnah, 136
suq, 37
Swan, 35
Swinburn, 38

—T—

talaq, 112
taqlīd, 15
tawhid, 19
ṭawāf al difāḍah, 23
ṭawāf al qudūm, 20

tax on wealth, 91
taxes, 17
tea
    green, 77
Tibi, 159
Tocqeville de, 164
Trinity, 39
Tworuschka, 143

—U—

'Uhud, 6
Ummah, 67, 136
Uz, 83

—V—

veil, 109
veil, facial, 108
virginity, 104
Vitray-Meyérovitch de, 133, 138
Vöcking, 143

—W—

washing, 26
weddings, 101
wine tastings, 56
Wischnewski, 120
women, 1, 2, 12, 13, 22
wuqūf, 21

—Z—

zakah, 91
Zayat el, 140
Zayed, 73
Zentralrat der Muslime in Deutschland, 148
Zullah, 25